The Poverty of Progressivism

The Poverty
of Progressivism

The Future of American Democracy
in a Time of Liberal Decline

Jeffrey C. Isaac

ROWMAN & LITTLEFIELD PUBLISHERS, INC.
Lanham • Boulder • New York • Oxford

ROWMAN & LITTLEFIELD PUBLISHERS, INC.

Published in the United States of America
by Rowman & Littlefield Publishers, Inc.
A Member of the Rowman & Littlefield Publishing Group
4720 Boston Way, Lanham, Maryland 20706
www.rowmanlittlefield.com

PO Box 317
Oxford
OX2 9RU, UK

British Library Cataloguing in Publication Information Available

Library of Congress Cataloging-in-Publication Data
Isaac, Jeffrey C., 1957–
    The poverty of progressivism : the future of American democracy in a time of
liberal decline / Jeffrey C. Isaac.
      p. cm.
    Includes bibliographical references and index.
    ISBN 0-7425-2324-1 (hardcover : alk. paper)—ISBN 0-7425-2325-X (pbk. : alk. paper)
      1. Conservatism—United States. 2. Progressivism (United States politics). 3. Democracy—
United States. 4. United States—Politics and Government—1989– I. Title.

JK27 .I72 2003
320.51'3'0973—dc21   2002009851

Printed in the United States of America

♾™ The paper used in this publication meets the minimum requirements of
American National Standard for Information Sciences—Permanence of Paper
for Printed Library Materials, ANSI/NISO Z39.48–1992.

For Lisi,
With Love and Edification

Contents

Acknowledgments

I have been working on this project for a long time, and during this time I have incurred a great many debts to the many colleagues, friends, and family members whose words and deeds have enriched my life.

I would like first to thank Mary Carpenter, editor at Rowman & Littlefield, and her two anonymous reviewers, for their help in making my book a better one.

I would also like to thank the following colleagues, who have either read parts of the manuscript or whose conversations have contributed to my thinking about this project or about politics more generally: Steven Ashby, Sorin Antohi, Christine Barbour, Rick Battistoni, Jack Bielasiak, Jason Bivins, Purnima Bose, Harry Boyte, Myles Brand, Maria Bucur, Joann Campbell, Mitchell Cohen, Aurelian Craiutu, E. J. Dionne Jr., Suzi Dovi, Stephen Elkin, Judy Failer, Matt Filner, Lew Friedland, Todd Gitlin, Jeffrey Gould, Russell Hanson, Miklos Haraszti, Bob Ivie, Danny James, John Judis, Ira Katznelson, Mark Levinson, Steven Lukes, Jenny Mansbridge, Kevin Mattson, Adam Michnik, Tun Myint, Ian Shapiro, Theda Skocpol, Michael Shuman, Carmen Sirianni, Dave Sprintzen, Phil Thompson, Tim Tilton, Vladimir Tismaneanu, Sue Tuohy, Michael Walzer, Jeffrey Wasserstrom, and Iris Marion Young.

I would like to thank the Lynde and Harry Bradley Foundation (special thanks to William Schambra) and the Open Society Institute (special thanks to Gail Goodman, Mark Schmitt, and Jo-Ann Mort) for their generous support of the research and writing that went into the production of this book. Special thanks also go to Morton Lowengrub, former Dean of the College of Arts and Science at Indiana University, and Kumble Subbuswamy, the current Dean of the College, for their support of my work.

My work as a teacher, writer, and political theorist has been enriched immeasurably by my public involvements in Bloomington, Indiana, the place that I am proud to call my home. I have both learned from and been inspired by my colleagues at Bloomington United: Doug Bauder, Beverly Calendar-Anderson, Josh Casares, Melanie Castillo-Cullather, John Clower, Bob Goldstein, Ruth Goldstein, C. J. Hawking, Steve Howard, Rebecca Jiminez, Elizabeth Lion, Dick McKaig, Barbara McKinney, Sue Shifron, Mira Wasserman, Jeffrey Willsey, and Charlotte Zietlow. My work with the Safe and Civil City Office of the City of Bloomington has been the source of much insight into the nature of civil society initiatives, and I would like to thank Marsha Bradford, the Director of that office, and Mayor John Fernandez for making this collaboration so satisfying. I would also like to note those with whom I have worked on the Indiana University Sweatshop Advisory Committee, especially Bennett Baumer, Purnima Bose, Lynn Duggan, Liz Feitl, Jacob Hannan, Megan Hise, Jenny McDaniel, Eduardo Rhodes, Al Ruesink, Damon Sims, Matt Turassini, and Dick McKaig, who has so ably chaired the committee.

As I have done in each of my books, and as I will do as long as I continue to write, I would like to thank those who have been and those who continue to be my teachers and mentors: Bob Dahl, Michael Harrington, Mike Krasner, Peter Manicas, Lennie Markovitz, Frank Warren, Mike Wreszin, Dennis Young, and Burt Zwiebach, with special thanks to Ray Franklin, whose friendship, advice, and conversation has enriched me immeasurably over the years.

I would like to thank the following for their friendship, which has helped to sustain me and my family over the years: Amy and John Applegate, Rich Balaban, Julie Bloom, Terry and Jerry Coleman, Ben Eisenstein, Carol Holton, Carolyn Lipson-Walker and George Walker, Andy and Jane Mallor, Steve and Linda Scott. Four friends deserve special mention. Casey Blake has been a kindred spirit, a supporter, and a source of invaluable insight ever since we both arrived together at Indiana University in 1987. While he has since moved on to Columbia University, he has remained for me an invaluable and dear conversation partner. Michael Walzer, who began for me as simply a luminary in my field, has become a trusted editor, who has opened the pages of *Dissent* magazine to me and has provided me with an intellectual home away from home. More than that, I have come to consider him a true interlocutor, an intellectual bellwether, and a friend. Over the past ten years or so my personal and intellectual life has been enriched immeasurably by my friendships with my dear friends Bob Orsi and John Efron. Our weekly breakfasts, and our many other occasions to talk and argue and laugh together, have been the source of pleasure, and intellectual stimulation and encouragement, beyond words. This year both left Bloomington; Bob to become Professor of Religion at the Harvard University Divinity School, and John to become Professor of History and Jewish Studies at University of California at Berkeley. I will miss them both, though I know our friendship will endure.

Finally, I offer my thanks to my family. My brother, Gary Isaac, and my sister-in-law, Toni Gilpin, are true intellectuals, whose conversation and kind words of support for my writing, have been important to me (it will not be long before their daughters, Amy and Esther, weigh in with their own words of wisdom on the affairs of the day). My aunt, Judith Silverstien, is an artist and poet who continues to inspire me. My parents, Sylvia and Hyman Isaac, have always been there for me, and for my family, with support and with love. I cannot thank them enough.

My wife, Debbie Kent, is quite simply the most amazing person I will ever know in this life. The acknowledgments of my books are like a running chronicle of her incredible accomplishments. Since my last book she has become the author of three commercially successful novels that are currently being considered by Hollywood producers, and in her spare time has become an accomplished stage designer and aficionado of "outsider art." She is also my rock, and my love. My son, Adam, is now a man, and his growth—physical, intellectual, emotional—has been a thing to behold. His toughness, his brilliance, and his talent—as a musician and as a cartoonist—continue to amaze and to inspire me. And then there is my daughter, Lisi. Lisi is, quite simply, a blessing. The beauty of her smile is matched only by the beauty of her heart. A superb student, an immensely talented performer, and a young lady with the courage of her convictions, she has been the source of much joy in my life and the life of our family. She has been waiting patiently for "her" book. I dedicate this one to her with much love.

Introduction

This book has been a long time coming. Indeed, it is hard for me to know exactly when I started writing it. I began developing its guiding theme back in 1995, in response to a wave of essays and books calling for and anticipating a revival of turn-of-the-century Progressivism as a solution to the current ills of American politics. That effort was eventually published in *Dissent* magazine as a 1996 essay entitled "The Poverty of Progressivism," and it generated a symposium and numerous exchanges from which I have learned much. But in fact many of the arguments contained in that essay were first broached in an even earlier *Dissent* piece, "Going Local," about the implications of the "Gingrich Revolution" of 1994. It is easy to forget, but that electoral event at the time had ground-shattering significance. The dramatic Democratic congressional defeat for many seemed to symbolize the depths to which liberalism had fallen in American public life, and the equally dramatic Republican victory seemed to betoken a groundswell of grassroots activism on behalf of conservative causes. Even then I did not consider this "Republican Revolution" as a realigning moment or as the beginning of a new age of conservative political dominance. But I was convinced that this development possessed deeper significance, and reflected a profound weakening of the support for organized liberalism.

It is this weakening of liberalism that is the principal focus of this book—its causes, its consequences, and its significance for thinking about "left liberal" politics in the United States. The label "left liberal," like all political labels today, requires clarification. By "left liberal" I mean that version of liberal politics in the United States most closely associated with the historical project of "the left," that is, the project of limiting and contesting the inequalities and injustices of capitalism, and of using the power of democratically legitimated governments to counter the power of wealthy and politically privileged elites. In American history the three great defining moments of such a left liberalism have been the Progressive era, the New Deal era, and the Great Society era. What I am here calling left liberalism has never been wholly coterminous with liberalism, for liberalism in the American context has always admitted more centrist or even conservative versions, which have reluctantly accommodated political reforms but have never truly been animated by reformist impulses. Indeed, it has not even been coterminous with liberal progressivism, understood as the most reformist and modernizing tendency within American liberalism. For at each moment in the development of American left liberalism in this century, progressive reforms have been fueled in large part by insurgent movements, to the "left," as it were, of the liberal mainstream, movements—such as Populism, or the IWW, or the radicalized industrial unions of the 1930s, or the "poor people's movements" of the 1960s—that operated outside the confines of party politics, that generated mass social unrest, and that articulated powerful and often angry criticisms of the political system itself. Such "left" movements typically understood themselves to be—and were taken to be—at odds with or at least challengers to liberalism. And liberals, even progressive liberals, typically saw their task to be the preemption and cooptation of such movements and their demands. By "left liberalism" I mean that complex and unstable coalescence of liberal progressivism and impulses and movements to the left of it that together worked to press for political change in the twentieth century.

One of the principal shortcomings of contemporary writers promoting a Progressive revival has been their failure to reckon with the past importance of such insurgent movements and with the current absence of similar or functionally equivalent ones. Yet such movements, whether purposefully or not, typically worked in tandem with Progressive liberal reformers who were interested in instituting the changes needed to cool things off, to satisfy popular agitation, and to make the system "work" more effectively. And the success of these reforms at each moment was a sign of the success of such a political division of labor. In this sense while left liberalism has not been coterminous with liberal Progressivism, liberal Progressivism has been the political centerweight, as it were, of left liberalism in America; it has been the functional equivalent of what in Europe has gone by the name of social democracy. It is the weakening of this Progressive centerweight that is the principal subject of this book.

In calling attention to the parallels with European social democracy, I mean to suggest that my inquiry has general implications for thinking about "the left" in the countries variously called "advanced capitalist" or "advanced industrial" or even "democratic"—countries possessing liberal democratic political systems, capitalist forms of private property, "welfare states," and postindustrial economies undergoing dramatic changes associated with such things as "third wave technological revolution" and "globalization." Current debates on the global left about the nature and limits of social democracy, and the political and economic rationales for new, "third way" policies, are closely linked to the issues discussed below. And aspects of my own argument about the poverty of progressivism in the United States have a broader relevance and help to explain why conventional social democratic responses may well be anachronistic, and so-called third way alternatives may be the most plausible forms of political response available to "left" governments. But my argument is nonetheless focused on the American case, because this is the case that I know best, and because, as an American academic and citizen, I am principally interested here in joining current debates about the future of American democracy, debates very much informed by specific historical understandings about the legacies of American Progressivism.

The Poverty of Progressivism is a short book consisting of four chapters on specific aspects of Progressivism, its current debilitation, and the effort to rehabilitate it. It is best read as an extended essay of historically informed political theory. While many writers have written about the revival of American democracy, and while many more have held forth about a Progressive revival, few have sought seriously to consider, in general terms, the broad historical similarities and dissimilarities between the current moment and the Progressive era, and to reflect intelligently on their meaning. This book is an effort to do just that, to examine the overall contours of twentieth-century American liberalism, to consider the reasons why this liberalism is in decline, and to identify signposts of the future, possible avenues through which generally left liberal values of political and social equality can be advanced under current conditions.

It is worth noting explicitly that the concept of "Progressivism" is itself a complex and contested category. While the idiom of neoprogressive political writing that concerns me in this book is a real and important genre of political commentary today, and hardly a function of my own imagination, it is nonetheless true that there is no single or univocal "Progressivism" in American politics. In Bloomington, Indiana, for example, where I live, there is a group of business advocates called Positive Progress that supports such self-styled "progressive" policies as the leasing of public spaces to private businesses, the privatization of public service delivery, and the dramatic retrenchment of zoning restrictions on private land development. This group draws no succor from any rhetorical similarity between its goals and those of turn-of-the-century Progressives, and indeed it is emphatically anti-Progressive in its political orientation. But it draws on a grammar of "progress" to articulate its faith in technological innovation and economic growth. Indeed, if there is any truth to the thesis of American exceptionalism, it is the relative absence of a powerful and truly reactionary conservative political tradition. In the American context some version of liberalism has always been hegemonic, and even the most "conservative" and social Darwinist of liberals have tended to speak the language of modernization and "progress."

Closer to the political home of neoprogressives, the Clinton administration from the outset relied heavily on appeals to "progressivism" in general and to the Progressivism of Roosevelt, Wilson, and Croly in particular. Indeed, there existed extremely close ties between the Clinton administration, the neoliberal Democratic Leadership Council cofounded by Clinton, its organ the Progressive Policy Institute run by Will Marshall, and such important neoprogressive intellectuals as Stanley Greenberg (Clinton's chief pollster in 1992), Robert Reich (Clinton's first Secretary of Labor), and E. J. Dionne Jr. (whose 1991 book, *Why Americans Hate Politics*, is sometimes considered a bible of early Clintonism). In each case the Clinton regime sought to draw upon or to use some theme associated with these intellectuals. Yet in each case this use turned out to be a misuse and perhaps an abuse, as a general rhetoric of progressivism was invoked to justify a profound scaling back of public policy ambition in the name of electoral and party-political success. Thus the literature of disenchantment, of which Reich's memoir *Locked in the Cabinet* is only the best-known example (others include Peter Edelman's recent *Searching for America's Heart* and Benjamin Barber's *The Truth of Power: Intellectual Affairs in the Clinton White House*).

Now there may have been good *realpolitik* reasons for such an exploitation of the rhetoric of "progressivism." Indeed, if the argument of this book is correct, then given current social conditions and the current balance of political forces, there is little reason to expect much more than this from the Democratic party or from the national political leadership of any other political party inclined to employ Progressive rhetoric, something I return to in the final chapter. Furthermore, in many ways the Clinton use of the rhetoric of progressivism is little different from the rhetoric of pro-business groups such as Positive Progress; like them, Clinton always articulated a profound faith in technological innovation and economic growth, and like them he stood for the "liberation" of the most up-to-date, forward-looking, "progressive" forces of production from the anachronistic constraints of "old-style," Progressive liberal government. In many ways the very success of Clinton as a master campaigner was due in no small part to his ability to meld this faith in technology and in third wave capitalism with a rhetoric of liberal progressive political concern and a policy agenda that substantially repudiates that concern *in the name of progress and modernization itself.*

This may be a recipe for political success. And it may represent an astute adaptation to current realities. But it is not what the neoprogressives that are the principal concern of this book have in mind. Their progressivism is more serious about social change and political reform, regulating the market, creating new opportunities through public policy, and limiting the power of entrenched elites. It is neither opportunistic political rhetoric nor technological window dressing nor a mere strategy of electoral victory. It is a credible and coherent substantive political orientation linked to a serious commitment to the realization of liberal values. These neoprogressives take themselves intellectually seriously. This is what warrants our attention, and warrants a serious consideration of their historical and strategic arguments, rather than a merely tactical or rhetorical analysis of how "progressive" rhetoric can be used—along with much money, opportunism, and good fortune—to win an election or two or three. For this reason I am little concerned in this book with Clintonism, except insofar as Clintonism is symptomatic of the decline of Progressive liberalism and perhaps also of the ill-fated hubris of well-meaning liberal intellectuals, who invested too much faith, and hope, in the possibilities presented by the 1992 victory of Clinton. I return, in the final chapter, to the theme of "the third way," and consider the ways in which its retreat from Progressive liberalism rests upon an accurate political diagnosis. But in no way is this intended as a rationale for the rhetorical opportunism that attended the policy agenda of the Clinton administration.

There is a famous and much-quoted aphorism from the Italian Marxist Antonio Gramsci, who observed that the old was dying, and the new was not yet born; at such historical watersheds, Gramsci wrote, numerous symptoms of "morbidity" appear. Like Gramsci, and like today's neoprogressives, I believe that our time is a time of transformation during which symptoms of morbidity—political alienation and cynicism, stark inequalities between rich and poor, urban decay and racial division, environmental degradation—abound. We are beyond the liberalism that had flourished since the 1930s, and that was inaugurated by Progressives earlier in the century. New technologies, and new forms of capital accumulation, seem to have both defied and outstripped old liberal forms of regulation; and yet we have not devised a new *political* (as opposed to technological or economic) settlement, a new way of processing and of solving the public problems thrown up by the new conditions. The neoprogressivism that concerns me in this book anticipates that the challenges and opportunities presented by the new economics—if properly understood and acted upon—will in time call forth such a settlement. I am skeptical. Indeed, this book can be viewed as an extended account of such skepticism. I support an optimism of neither the intellect nor the will, but rather a more chastened and skeptical ethos and a more fragmented and improvisational politics that anticipates no large or "hegemonic" way of resolving the problems that confront us. While neoprogressives anticipate, hope for, and work toward a new synthesis that moves us beyond our current morbidities, I am much less politically hopeful. As I see it political *stasis* is as likely a scenario for the short to medium term as is political progress; indeed, the political meaning of stasis is a main theme of the book's concluding sections, and the underlying concern of the book itself. In nature, at least as we have experienced it thus far, dawn follows dusk. But there is no reason to believe that the same is necessarily true in politics.

It is worth pointing out that there is a difference between skepticism and pessimism. For in politics pessimism of even the most studied variety typically counsels despair or at least a certain hopelessness about the possibilities of change. The skepticism exemplified and defended in this book does not counsel either. It simply counsels a healthy, realistic, pragmatic sense of the limiting and frustrating possibilities that currently present themselves. An acknowledgment of this does not entail or require resignation or passive acceptance of the status quo. But it does require a new political sensibility, one at home on the margins of the system, working against particular injustices, pursuing creative and improvisational policy responses in the absence of either a totalizing alternative or an oppositional mass politics. Such a sensibility allows us to express our indignation, to grope for alternatives, and to take inspiration and draw hope from successful efforts to improve our world, but without the hope of One Big Alternative or even of one coherent, "progressive" political agenda or organized political purpose.

There are good reasons why such a position is rarely articulated publicly on the left. For on the one hand such a position offers little inspiration for those activists who seek to challenge the existing political system or even aspects of it, who would prefer a more buoyant and heroic rhetoric of opposition or reform, and who perhaps require such a self-image in order to work with such dedication against great odds. And, on the other hand, such a view is too nuanced, too ambivalent, too qualified to gain a hearing in the melodramatic world of postmodern publicity, a world of simplicities and cynicisms, of slogans and celebrities. The kind of skepticism I advance in this book offers little comfort or inspiration. And it suffers from its own drawbacks, the most powerful of which is the ever-present danger of falling into a unique form of cynicism, whereby every unsuccessful effort to effect ambitious social change is met by a knowing "I told you so." This danger needs to be honestly acknowledged, and it is my hope in this book to keep it at bay. For the very same realism that urges caution also urges an experimental openness to latent and emergent possibilities that may present themselves. Indeed, if this book has a prejudice, it is the belief that such a pragmatic and experimental realism is indispensable for discerning, and appreciating, the opportunities for change that actually do exist, and for intelligently informing citizens in their efforts to realize these possibilities.

In this sense the book exemplifies, or at least seeks to exemplify, a distinctive kind of democratic pragmatism. There has been a remarkable revival of pragmatism in political theory and the humanities in recent years, and this book is very much intended as a contribution to such a revival. In political theory this revival of pragmatism has been linked to a number of distinct but related literatures that have sought to address the kinds of issues that lie at the heart of this book. One such literature is the discourse of "communitarianism" that began as a response to the arguments of liberal academic philosophers such as John Rawls and Bruce Ackerman, and evolved into a broader discussion of the limits of individualism, whether this be the individualism of the capitalist market or of the bureaucratic welfare state and its clientelistic relationships. This communitarianism has placed questions of locality, character formation, and civic virtue at the heart of its concern, and has argued that the generation of new forms of solidarity and responsibility is the central challenge facing American democracy today. Michael Sandel's book *Democracy's Discontent* is the most sustained and cogent statement of this view, and there are many overlaps between its concerns and those developed in this book (in the final chapter, I critically appraise Sandel's eloquent call for a "new public philosophy").

This literature converges with a second literature that has broached similar themes—the literature on "social capital" and "civil society." Robert Putnam's *Bowling Alone* is the most well-known contribution to this genre but, truth be told, this concern with "social" or "moral capital" and with the cultivation of civil society and its intermediate institutions, with a special focus on family, religious congregation, and neighborhood, has been a staple of neoconservative discourse for decades. The current literature is by no means reducible to neoconservatism; but it sounds themes regarding the limits of social policy and the importance of civic solidarities that have long been articulated by critics of the welfare state. What distinguishes current discussions is a great sense of urgency, and a heightened attention to matters not simply of moral relevance but of policy relevance as well, regarding the "third sector" and new forms of civic initiative and social service delivery. Carmen Sirianni and Lewis Friedland's recently published book *Civic Innovation in America* beautifully summarizes and extends this discourse, and I turn to their argument in the concluding chapter.

There is, finally, the growing body of work in political theory on the subject of "deliberative democracy." This literature, like the others mentioned earlier, thematizes serious problems of democratic legitimacy plaguing American society. This literature is immense. Probably the most widely cited contribution is Amy Guttman and Dennis Thompson's *Democracy and Disagreement*. Like the other genres, with which it is obviously linked, this literature emphasizes alternatives to existing party-political and state institutions, underscoring the importance of more accessible and authentic forms of civic participation and dialogue. But this literature is distinguished by its explicit attention to the norms and requisites of democratic citizenship and deliberation, and by its emphasis on forms of communication and negotiation of disagreement and difference that might enhance the legitimacy of public institutions and decisions.

It is probably not an exaggeration to say that these literatures are the three principal genres of American political theory today. Each of them is at least in part driven by the effort to address the defects of current political arrangements such as political alienation, privatism, and cynicism about public life. And each of them is linked with the effort to revive pragmatism broadly construed. This is true in terms of historical exemplars, and also in terms of the broadly pragmatic and applied thrust of much of this literature, which goes beyond narrowly academic concerns and seeks a broader audience of concerned citizens and civic leaders. This public orientation no doubt helps to explain why these discussions have attracted extraordinary attention and generous financial support from a range of foundations and philanthropies, from the avowedly liberal Open Society Institute of the Soros Foundation to the more centrist Pew Charitable Trusts and Kettering Foundations, to the conservative Lynde and Harry Bradley Foundation.

These literatures attest to the challenges confronting democratic political theory today, and to the fact that these challenges are being taken up by concerned and engaged scholars across the political spectrum. At the same time, it seems to me that these literatures, even though they address genuine issues and often support quite specific practical solutions, like deliberative polling techniques or community development corporations, are insufficiently attentive to the *political* character of the problems they address. While they typically assume a narrowly pragmatic stance, seeking "solutions" to perceived problems, what is missing from most of these accounts are explicit discussions of the distributions of wealth and power and broad consideration of the profound historical and structural changes currently underway in the United States and in the broader world. There is something abstract and formulaic about many of these discussions, as if problems of legitimacy and civic engagement can be considered apart from a consideration of the history of organized liberalism and the breakdown of the liberal regime, and as if the right moral appeal or the proper dialogic technique can substitute for *politics*, in all of its messiness, contentiousness, and frustration. This book is distinguished by its explicit attention to political issues such as these. While I too believe that American democracy confronts serious challenges, and that innovations in civil society and public discourse can help to address these challenges, I believe that these matters cannot be considered in isolation from a consideration of the broad political and economic environment and the opportunities for experimentation and reform that it affords. And my analysis of this environment makes me skeptical about much that is proposed by way of "solutions," because these proposals are too often credulous about the flexibility of political and economic institutions and indifferent to serious obstacles in the way of meaningful political change. They are, in a word, insufficiently strategic. And a political theory that is indifferent to questions of strategy is a political theory that courts irrelevance and, when taken seriously and acted upon, courts frustration, or worse.

This book is written in a pragmatic spirit that is more strategic and political. A complete delineation and defense of this pragmatism would require another book or at least turn this into a very different kind of book, more akin to a book of academic political philosophy. Such an account will have to await another occasion. For I am here concerned primarily with the programmatics of American liberalism and with programmatic discussions of the future of this liberalism. Nonetheless I do think it would be helpful to outline some of the basic assumptions underlying my critical account of Progressivism and its impoverishment.

The first is that all human practices and institutions are artificial, the product of human agency or, more properly, of multiple human agencies, under definite, complex, and changing historical conditions. There is nothing given or inalterable about human arrangements. This claim may seem fairly commonplace. But in fact it has serious implications. On the one hand, it stands against the widespread belief in the quasi-natural status of market and family institutions, a belief first conveyed to me, long ago, by a teacher who explained to me that "that's just the way things are." This belief in the inalterability of existing practices, of course, is still predominant in our society, and it has played no small role in justifying the attack on "liberal social engineering" and the retrenchment of welfare state policies that has dominated the last two decades. On the other hand, the above-stated assumption regarding the complexity of social practices cuts against the naive idea, often held by "progressives" of various stripes, that it is possible to capture of the essence of, and thus to "master," the unfolding historical process. This view is equally naive, because it fails to see that "society" is a complex and shifting target of intervention and also that it is the product of multiple agencies. The dream of a single agency capable of bringing history to heel, of resolving antagonisms and setting things right, is a dangerous and hopeless one. The world is *not* too complex to be creatively and beneficially changed; but it is far too complex for us to have any confidence in *that* conception of progressive change. For it does not follow from the fact that the social world is artificial and historical that we can muster up a collective purposiveness capable, in the words of the early Walter Lippmann, of transforming "drift" into "mastery."

Second, reason is not simply a "Western" phenomenon, as some cultural critics would have it, or merely a scholarly phenomenon, the province of certified professionals, as some self-assured and insulated academics (and some of their anti-intellectual critics) would have it. Reasoning is a historically evolved *human and social* capacity to reflect on the world and to understand and cope with practical problems of human living. Such reasoning can take and has taken many forms; and it has always confronted profound intellectual and political obstacles. But in the modern world such reasoning has managed to find certain niches and to assume a certain precarious prominence. And to the good. For critical inquiry into the sources of practical problems and their possible solutions is indispensable to human thriving; and the alternative to such inquiry is not some more authentic mode of being but simply superstition, myth, habit, *and unexamined and unquestioned power*. This insight was the basis of the Enlightenment, and of the "age of democratic revolutions" that the Enlightenment helped to spawn, as it has been the basis of every important democratizing movement of modern times. Democracy is indeed the political arrangement that best realizes this insight, because it allows for the free production and dissemination of critical ideas, and affords citizens the right to act on their beliefs to question and contest the terms of their social engagements.

The history of democratic argument, and the history of democracy itself, as an idea and as a practice, is no doubt complicated. Democracy is both a contested concept and a complex and flawed form of politics. It is not perfect, either in conception or in operation. Indeed, the form of political democracy under which we live is highly truncated, characterized by many kinds of inequality, limited by many kinds of corruption and immobilism. Nonetheless the civil and political freedoms afforded to citizens by this political democracy make possible numerous forms of political critique and contestation, and these in turn make possible the formation of political associations and organizations capable of at least somewhat effecting popular demands and holding public policy accountable to these demands. This is no small matter, as the dark history of the twentieth century attests. Another way of putting this is that democracy has been an indispensable political means of advancing claims of justice;

and that the achievements in justice that were enacted in the previous century were very much the outcomes of democratic political contestation.

This needs to be kept at the forefront of any serious discussion of Progressivism and its limits today. And it is something often forgotten both by conservatives, who wrongly ignore this and blame these achievements on arrogant "liberal elites," thereby obscuring the popular sources of twentieth-century progressivism; and by liberals, who imagine that if they can only figure out the right argumentative technique or theory of distributive justice or policy innovation or political formula then the public will be disposed readily to fall into line and we will again be set on the road to progress. What both of these views—one hostile toward Progressivism, the other hopeful—fail to see is that democratic politics makes possible contestation of existing arrangements, and indeed such contestations acquire legitimacy through democratic means; but democracy does *not* make such contestations necessary or inevitable nor, of course, does it assure anything about their possible outcomes should they emerge.

Thus, while inquiring and questioning is the essence of pragmatism, and democracy, on my understanding of pragmatism, is the best political means of enhancing such inquiry and questioning, this questioning is not a mere academic or intellectual phenomenon, and it does not take place in a social or political vacuum. All questioning and all contestation takes place amidst an existing institutional setting and an existing distribution of money, power, and access to the means of communication. For this reason pragmatic theorizing about democracy and its future possibilities is best conceived as *strategic* theorizing, theorizing not simply about ideals or about ingenious or desirable alternatives but about existing challenges and emergent probabilities. It is to such strategic thinking that this book seeks to contribute.

Fourth, in thinking strategically, I endorse, and hope to apply, a generally experimental approach to power, rejecting dogmatic attachments to markets or states, but also rejecting the dogmatic vilification of either markets or states. Much of the rhetoric of the right in the United States clearly embraces markets and disparages states; and on the left there are many—especially vocal during the recent protests against the WTO and World Bank in Seattle and Washington, D.C.—who disparage markets and private corporations and envision some kind of global anticorporate alternative, presumably relying on powerful state or quasi-state constraints on economic activity. As a pragmatist I am suspicious of both perspectives, precisely because they are both too categorical. For the right, power is held by the state and it needs to be displaced; and, for much of the left, power is held by corporate capital, and it, similarly, needs to be unseated or displaced. There is, of course, truth to both claims. Since the early Progressive era over a century ago, the American state has assumed important regulatory powers. And, of course, while these powers have constrained private capital, they have never supplanted it. Indeed, as I think I have already made clear, if I am wary of both oversimplifications, I am much more wary of the first, for it obscures both the power of corporate capital and the historical indispensability of state regulation both to the continued flourishing of this power *and* to the tempering and thus the humanization of this power. Nonetheless at the level of politics and policy both simplifications are simplifications, and as such they are to be avoided. For "power" does not lie in a single, unambiguous, and easily locatable place; nor is it something that can readily be unseated, displaced, or somehow transcended. Rather, the American system for the past century has been characterized by a complicated combination of public and private powers. And, for a variety of reasons, only some of which I discuss below, it is not realistic to imagine that in the next century it will be possible to do away with governmental regulation or corporate capital or private markets.

Strategic thinking should thus be focused on how the balance between these institutions might be reconfigured and on the probable agencies of such a reconfiguration. Much of the literature of neoprogressivism that I criticize in this book is so focused. And while I take issue with many aspects of this literature, I believe that most of its proponents are motivated by a pragmatic sensibility akin to the one I have delineated. My disagreements with them derive not from the absence of serious, nuanced programmatic arguments in their work, but rather from my sense of the *limitations* of these arguments, which are to my mind too hopeful, too credulous about the prospects for a profound revival of organized liberalism. But there is clearly no single way to think about these questions, and much of what I argue is thus evidently contestable. Indeed, all such arguments are necessarily hypothetical and, by calling attention to experimentalism, I mean to highlight just this fact. There really is no way to know how the political and economic history of the future will unfold. And there are no doubt alternative trajectories that greatly depend on how people choose to interpret the world and then act on these interpretations. It is thus wise to approach the subject of the future of American liberalism with a healthy and experimental sense of the openness of history.

Nonetheless, two caveats are in order regarding such an experimental attitude. First, practical "experiments" always take place in a limiting context and, if it is mistaken to assume a dogmatic attitude toward what is possible and what might work, it is equally mistaken to become so enamored of the powers of human agency that one ignores the existence of trends, tendencies, and institutions of power that limit, even if they do not strictly determine, what is possible. Indeed, the biggest weakness of much pragmatist theorizing, going back to the writings of Dewey himself, has been a kind of fetishized "experimentalism" that is really unpragmatic precisely because it ignores broad questions of power. Social life is not a game or a controlled experiment, and political agents are not detached or specialized scientists seeking to discern law-like relations between events or to contrive ingenious solutions to intellectual puzzles. The kinds of experiments that are possible and meaningful in politics are undertaken under duress, in problematic situations of social living that disturb complacency and that require some kind of response in the name of practicality—in order to keep a job, or a home, or to be able to live where one chooses, or to have clean drinking water for oneself and one's children. And these "experiments," furthermore, take place not in a laboratory but in a social world laced with power, and historical grievances, resentments, and antagonisms; and one's experimental efforts always come up against the projects of others and also against sedimented assumptions and institutionalized patterns that privilege some projects over others.

The second caveat is that while it is important to understand and to theorize about this limiting context, such limitations should not be overtheorized, for while they truly are constraining, they never are determinative. There is always room for maneuver, always the possibility of the occurrence of the unanticipated. The East German Communist regime might not have opened the borders to Hungary, setting in motion a tidal wave of change in Eastern Europe; but it did. Indeed, much of the change brought about by the Eastern European "Revolutions of 1989" was utterly unanticipated, in some ways virtually miraculous. Similarly, Martin Luther King Jr. might not have decided to return to Birmingham, Alabama, in 1963; but he did, and the civil rights movement maintained a momentum that it might otherwise have lost. There is no way to predict developments such as these. Of course, behind them are broader historical forces. But these forces are operative, as it were, only through human agency. And unanticipated human decisions such as the ones mentioned above open up genuine historical possibilities that might otherwise not ever present themselves. For this reason it is a mistake to attribute too much coherence and too much power to prevailing institutions, for there are always openings, even if small ones, in the fabric of the present. And for this reason all arguments about progressivism, liberalism, and the future of democracy in America—including my own—can be no more than hypotheses and should forswear an attitude of certainty or excessive confidence.

Finally, pragmatist theorizing today ought to be preeminently self-reflexive, and thus painfully aware of the practical limits of even the most cogent analysis and argument. For political inquiry and argument is profoundly constrained, on the one hand by the structure and ethos of the dominant means of communication—the politics of the mass media—which shape, select, and limit what can be argued and how it can be conveyed, and on the other hand by the sociology of mass audiences, and by the very real mundane concerns, and media distractions, that occupy the attentions of ordinary Americans, and make it so difficult to inject critical arguments into broad public debate. Indeed, this factor is a main subtheme of this book. For the greatest failing of many neoprogressives is their failure to take sufficient account of the media institutions that limit the dissemination of a "progressive" message and the formation of committed progressive publics.

In each of these respects my argument has close affinities with two recent books similarly developing a pragmatist approach to the problems of democratic politics today: Roberto Mangabiera Unger and Cornel West's *The Future of American Progressivism: An Initiative for Political and Economic Reform* (1998) and Unger's more theoretical *Democracy Realized: The Progressive Alternative* (1998). Both of these books take their bearings from the impasse of organized liberalism, and both endorse an "experimental" approach to markets and states and a participatory democratic politics centered in civil society. There is much programmatic overlap between these books and my own. But Unger and West exhibit a much more powerful faith in "experimentalism," a faith that, in my view, often blinds them to questions of power. There is, moreover, a hortatory and almost prophetic tone to these books, one no doubt due in part to West's own "prophetic" persona, but also, I think, to the particular influence of Richard Rorty upon the version of pragmatism that they endorse. For these books can be read as the programmatic companions to Rorty's own powerful essay *Achieving Our Country: Leftist Thought in Twentieth Century America*. In this short book Rorty extols an unabashed pride in "the American experiment" and endorses a liberalism of "pure joyous hope." His argument centers on the figure of Walt Whitman, democratic writer par excellence. Whitman, on Rorty's reading, is not simply the poet of American self-identity; he is something of a prophet who saw that "the United States are themselves the greatest poem," an artistic creation still in the process of becoming a truly existential nation: "our essence is our existence, and our existence is in the future." Rorty more than any other pragmatist writer views American history as a story of freedom that we continue to tell ourselves; and for him some version of left liberalism is simply the best, most hopeful story that can be told. Rorty's pragmatism is thus unashamedly romantic and indeed utopian; and there are similar traces of romanticism present in the Unger and West volume. But what is lacking in these endorsements of "experimentalism" is a sufficient appreciation of the obstacles confronting experimentalism, sufficient attention to those endemic features of American society that are not "poetic." For of course the

United States is not a poem, and the American existence does not precede its essence, and its destiny is not the future, Rorty's eloquence notwithstanding.

The Poverty of Progressivism is a book about the reasons why such an optimism is profoundly misplaced, and about why a more chastened, cautious, and genuinely pragmatic politics is probably the most promising way to navigate our way through the political immobilism in which American democracy finds itself. Its purpose is not to hearten, uplift, or inspire but to elucidate. But while it forswears a Rortyean optimism of "pure joyous hope," it is nonetheless hopeful that by elucidating it may also offer indications of creative possibility, and thus, in a small way, provide some measure of inspiration for citizens who are disheartened with the prevailing tendencies of American society and who wish to realize and extend democratic ideals.

The guiding spirit behind such an endeavor is Camusian. Albert Camus once wrote that he was "pessimistic as to mankind but optimistic as to man." I take him to have meant by this that while he was wary of unadulterated hopefulness or of grandiose visions of political liberation or reform, he was nonetheless hopeful about the capacity of human beings, in specific times and places, under duress and confronting limitations in themselves and in their world, to act with integrity, and ingenuity, to make their world a more habitable place. It is such a hopefulness that this book seeks to abet.

1

✛

The Progressive Revival

The conventional wisdom in America is that we are currently living amidst unparalleled progress and prosperity. Yet it is also impossible to ignore ever-present public discussion of various "malaises" befalling American society and, beneath this discussion, a widespread awareness, sometimes quite explicit, sometimes implicit, that American society is in the midst of a major transformation. The so-called social contract that had long governed American politics since the end of the Second World War has clearly broken down. The public policy arrangements comprising this "contract"—a system of "universal" social security broadly construed, a more or less orderly system of corporate labor relations, a cooptive and mildly reformist social policy designed to ameliorate racial antagonisms and urban problems—are all to one extent or another in serious disrepair and disrepute. And the political coalition that supported these arrangements—the so-called politics of the "Vital Center," a largely bipartisan politics dominated by the Democratic party—is clearly disrupted and demoralized. The consequences of this breakdown have been widely acknowledged by commentators for at least a decade—social decay, incessant ideological posturing and symbolic antagonism, and government immobilism. They are well summed up in the title of E. J. Dionne Jr.'s widely acclaimed 1991 book on the subject—*Why Americans Hate Politics*—a book that, while over a decade old, is still frequently cited as having captured an enduring truth about our contemporary political life.

That Americans do hate politics, or at least find it a distasteful and unworthy enterprise, cannot be doubted. Decreasing numbers of citizens turn out for elections. Public opinion polls register a disturbing lack of confidence in politicians, political parties, and governmental institutions. Political scientists write—with great public fanfare—about the strange disappearance of civic America, the vices of solitary bowling, and a growing isolation and disengagement from public life. The headlines widely and loudly proclaim a political restiveness and anxiousness among the citizenry, many of whom feel ill served by the existing arrangements, in spite of the recent unprecedented economic growth and stock market boom. Meanwhile, instead of serious debate, public discourse descends into image-mongering, partisan cant, character assassination, and chattering punditry about matters of secondary or even tertiary importance. And when not characterized by nastiness, public discourse is simply bland and boring. The body politic is not faring well.

This is not a problem only for liberals. Indeed, it is a problem for all Americans who care about democracy or simply care about the quality of their lives and the lives of their children. No one can afford to be complacent about the character and vitality of our political life. Yet the enervation of public life is a particular problem for liberalism, and for two reasons. First, for most of the twentieth century the dominant public philosophy in America has been some version of Progressive liberalism, and thus the political impasse that is upon us deeply implicates liberalism and its limitations. The "social contract" that is now dead and still being buried is a product of liberal politics, and its unravelling, and its evident lack of popularity, presents a serious challenge to liberalism. Can liberalism formulate a new public philosophy capable of addressing the problems of the twenty-first century? Can liberals restore public confidence in the problem-solving abilities of government? Such questions truly are pressing.

Second, the general antipathy toward politics that characterizes public life is a distinctive problem for liberalism because liberalism is or at least until recently has been an emphatically *public* philosophy, a philosophy committed to the existence of a robust public sector charged with the responsibility for promoting social and economic welfare. Without some kind of vigorous public life it is hard to see how there can be any meaningful kind of contemporary liberalism.

The same cannot be said for conservatism broadly understood, for the conservative movement has sought over the past four decades—with great success—to diminish the public sphere, to dismantle the public sector, to privatize governmental functions, and to promote a certain conception of liberty according to which individuals are free only when their families and their property are unencumbered by law or politics. Except, that is, if they are drug users, criminals, or others deemed somehow abnormal, deviant, or threatening to society, in which case the answer is more police and more prisons ("Extreme measures in the name of liberty are no vice . . . "). For most conservatives the current delegitimation of public life is not a problem at all but rather a promising response to the excessive governmentalism of twentieth-century liberalism. Indeed, one can go further and suggest that the delegitimation of public life marks the fulfillment of the conservative agenda, which has sought precisely this outcome—though not necessarily all of its unintended consequences.

In this regard Ronald Reagan truly was one of the "greatest" presidents of the twentieth century. For in the twelve years of the Reagan-Bush administration a new tone was set in public life—a tone of militant antigovernmentalism. The Reagan rhetoric of private liberty was deeply deceptive to be sure. Under its cover the nation's budget deficit soared; the police powers of the federal government were enhanced, and a boom in prison construction was inaugurated; corporate conglomeration flourished; and increased military expenditures supported a hawkish foreign policy designed to turn back the "Vietnam syndrome" and to play nuclear and economic "chicken" with the Soviet Union. Furthermore, most of the core institutions of the postwar welfare state—Social Security, Medicaid, the Department of Housing and Urban Development, the National Labor Relations Board, the Occupational Safety and Health Administration, the Environmental Protection Agency—remained intact, the best laid plans of James Watt, Rita Lavelle, and other conservative heroes of the Reagan era notwithstanding. Reagan did not return the country to the Tocquevillean, pastoral, freeholding paradise that his rhetoric often invoked. Nor, truth be told, did he ever really seek to do so; for, while the rhetoric retained much power, it was consistent neither with what most Americans—including his most conservative supporters—really wanted nor with what a modern political economy required.

Nonetheless the antigovernment rhetoric of what has come to be called "Reaganism" was powerful and effective, especially when backed up by a public policy agenda of retrenchment and dismantlement of the welfare state. Federal social programs were declared anathema to freedom and prosperity. The poor were continuously disparaged for their dependence, and liberal reformers, social service providers, and legal services advocates were demonized—and defunded—as corrupt oppressors of both rich *and* poor, and New Class elitists. Federal regulation of health and safety standards, of corporate transactions, and of the financial sector was condemned. Hostile administrators were appointed to head major federal agencies; investigatory staffs were downsized; narrow standards of economic cost-efficiency were put into place. While the Reagan-Bush regime did not literally undo the institutions of the postwar welfare state, it did declare them illegitimate and commit itself to a moratorium on further federal support for them. The message of these years was clear—the federal government, and indeed government more generally, is not part of the solution to our public problems but is itself the principal source of our problems.

In George Orwell's allegorical novella *Animal Farm*, the revolutionary pigs devise the simplistic slogan "four legs good, two legs bad" to mobilize opposition to the oppressive farmer Jones and his human compatriots. In the course of the narrative this slogan is continually manipulated, reinterpreted, and eventually revised as it suits the power of the swinish revolutionary vanguard. But the impulse behind the slogan continues to energize even in the face of the slogan's manifest inadequacy. For it is a simple slogan, easily repeated, and appealing to a mass of "citizens" reduced to spectatorship. In the Reagan years a similar slogan was devised and continually repeated by the greatest of "communicators" himself: "private life good, public life bad."

This slogan remains the ideological mantra of our times. While the slogan has never described reality, it has helped to *transform* reality, by delegitimizing social policy and indeed by repudiating the liberal project of constructive public policy that dominated American politics for most of the twentieth century. The power of this rhetoric, and of the policies of cutback that accompanied it, has been profound and immeasurable. For this discourse is the only public discourse that our young people have ever heard, and it is, to all appearances, the discourse of the future. It is spoken by the Republicans who have come to dominate the public policy agenda, but also by more and more Democrats who have abandoned even a notional commitment to "liberalism" in the name of the new "realism." We live, after all, in an era in which "welfare as we know it" has ceased to exist, in which unrestrained global trade is publicly unquestioned by the leaderships of both major parties and by the mass media, in which the forces of "third wave" economic transformation are considered in need of liberation from unwanted and intrusive, liberal, interference— and all this was heralded by a Democratic president! According to the new dispensation, government activity—especially when undertaken by so-called Big Government—is an "interference" to be avoided whenever possible. And public life is something to be minimized in the interests of money or celebrity or travel on the information superhighway. There are, to be sure, disagreements about the extent of market freedom that is desirable and about the extent to which Progressive liberalism is a culpable and anachronistic philosophy. The Clinton-Gore regime clearly supported certain policies—tepid health care reform, increases in federal expenditures for education, a small increase in the minimum wage, a modest Earned Income Tax Credit designed to assist some of the working poor— that have long been anathema to most Republicans. And it rhetorically embraced a conception of "progressivism"—though emphatically not any version of *liberalism*. But these partisan differences exist at the margins of what is undoubtedly a new party-political consensus about the unlimited opportunities presented by unrestrained global capitalism, a consensus marked by an unqualified enthusiasm about the stock market, Alan Greenspan, and the Internet.[1] Is it any wonder that in a society dominated by this idea there would be a suspicion of politics and a "disappearance of civic America"? Such a development might be disturbing, but it surely is not strange.

Yet it would be an error to attribute responsibility to conservatism for the breakdown of the "social contract" and of liberalism more generally, or to blame conservatives for the enervation of public life today. For these developments are the result of many forces, some of them long-term historical forces, over which both conservatives and liberals have had little control. Progressive liberalism in its ascendancy was propelled by powerful social and economic energies, and its demise was hastened by the depletion of those energies, by the often unintended negative consequences of liberal social policy, and by the generation of new powers not easily harnessed by liberalism. In many ways the conservative repudiation of liberalism simply announced certain emergent trends—political, economic, cultural—that had already weakened liberalism, trends that were themselves preconditions of the conservative ascendancy of the 1980s. Conservatism and its antigovernmental philosophy, then, are less the problem than the *symptom* of the problem. The problem is simple—and it is liberalism itself. The problem is the long-term impoverishment of Progressive liberalism, an impoverishment of political will and an impoverishment of political vision. Has Progressive liberalism ceased to be a relevant public philosophy? How might it be reconceived and revitalized? Can it be revitalized? These are the questions that guide this book. And the answers are not heartening.

THE IMPASSE OF LIBERALISM

It is worth underscoring that a focus on the disheartening enervation of Progressive liberalism is not the only way in which a discussion of the malaise of public life today might be framed. A variety of alternatives present themselves. One is simply to deny that there is a real problem worth discussing. Americans may be dissatisfied, it might be said, but most Americans have always been dissatisfied, for dissatisfaction is perhaps the most universal human experience. Public policy is deficient, but this too is a chronic problem. For, as the knowing economists and political scientists who dominate our university social science departments will tell us, public choice is always suboptimal. The dominant political parties are entrenched, corrupt, and disconnected from

core constituencies and the electorate at large, but this is a cardinal feature of advanced liberal democracies, and in no way impairs the func-
tioning of the competitive electoral system. The system of competitive
partisan elections is surely the worst system, except for all others.[2] The
economy presents problems of adjustment and maldistribution, but
that is the nature of capitalism. And however disorienting it is, capitalism has surely proven itself superior to all conceivable alternatives.[3]
From this point of view, it is pointless to wring one's hands about crises
of legitimacy, political impasses, or historic watersheds. For this is the
way the system works, this is the way it always has worked, and this is
the way it will continue to work, with results that are far from optimal
but also far short of deplorable.

Such a perspective is not without virtues. It surely represents a healthy,
realistic antidote to ritualistic evocations of crisis and catastrophe, for it is
true that American society today is far from collapse, and indeed many
Americans by all appearances are experiencing at least some measure of
prosperity and, whether prosperous or not, some measure of satisfaction
(here the power of easy credit and of TV should never be underestimated). But its main virtue is that it offers consolation. It invites us to
abandon whatever anxieties and doubts we may have about our common
world and to resign ourselves to the fact that ours is the best of all possible worlds. And isn't this posture confirmed by the still recent experience
of Communism's decline? For doesn't this demonstrate that we have
reached an "end of history" or at least an end of ideology, that our current
hybrid of representative democracy and corporate capitalism is the highest and freest form of social existence available to denizens of the world
on the cusp of the new millennium?

There are many problems with such a conclusion, but the most significant is that it lacks current resonance; it is, quite simply *unconvincing*. It is
noteworthy in this regard that Francis Fukuyama, whose 1989 essay "The
End of History" gave powerful expression to this discourse of consolation, has more recently turned in his writings to the subject of "trust," to
the importance of the moral resources and civic energies located in civil
society, and to the dangers associated with their current depletion in societies like our own. The shift in Fukuyama's own focus mirrors a broader
shift in public intellectual discourse. For if the heady transformations of
1989 gave credence to the sense that we really ought to celebrate the
achievements of liberal democratic societies like our own, subsequent developments have disturbed this sense of complacency. As Charles Meier
insisted a few years back in *Foreign Affairs*—a journal of mainstream elite
opinion, published by the Council on Foreign Relations—the advanced
liberal democracies confront nothing less than a "moral crisis," a crisis of
purpose and of political identity.[4] This sense is particularly evident

among intellectuals in the United States, which is perhaps one reason why the work of Robert Putnam has received so much attention. Putnam, indeed, is the only political scientist of which I am aware ever to have merited a feature story in *People* magazine! And the concerns about "social capital" and civic engagement that his work articulates have become staples not simply of liberal but of conservative periodicals as well, and the preoccupations of foundations and think tanks liberal and conservative. For they speak to widespread anxieties.

This leads me to another way of framing the problem, to which I have already alluded above—the conservative perspective broadly understood. On this view, the demise of liberalism is actually something to be celebrated as a liberation rather than bemoaned as a crisis of political identity. On this view antigovernmentalism, especially when linked to a conservative agenda of gutting the welfare state, is a healthy response to the manifest failures of liberal Progressivism, the perverse effects of its interventions in social life, its bureaucratic hostility toward civil society, the arrogance of its social engineering intellectuals, etc., etc. What America needs, on this view, is a political retrenchment combined with a moral renewal—a renaissance of bourgeois virtue, self-reliant entrepreneurial energy, family values of parental responsibility and restrained sexuality, and a healthy spirit of voluntarism, charitable contribution, and good works. And such a moral renewal, on this view, requires not simply a surpassing but a repudiation of Progressive liberalism.[5]

This viewpoint comes in two variants—the militant moralism of William Bennett, Robert Bork, Pat Buchanan, James Dobson, and others intent on waging a cultural/religious war for the "soul" of America; and a more nuanced insistence on the importance of civil society and social responsibility articulated in journals such as *Policy Review* by figures like former U.S. Senator Dan Coats, Michael Joyce, William Schambra, and Robert Woodson. There are important differences between these variants of conservative moralism. Conservative celebrants of civil society offer some intelligent criticisms of the bureaucratism that has characterized and impoverished Progressive liberalism and of the crass commercialism of mass mediated popular culture; and in their understanding of the importance of intermediate institutions between markets and states these writers are participants in an important conversation about the structure of a postliberal America. If conservative militants seem content to demonize liberalism, these other conservative writers take seriously the problem of social responsibility and the need to nourish social supports for such responsibility. Yet, as conservatives, these writers too tend toward a dogmatic antistatism. For them the liberal state—through its interference with the market but even more through its social policies on behalf of racial, gender, and sexual equality, which threaten traditional "family values"—is the principal source of corruption and oppression, and liberation from this state is the central problem of political life today.[6]

In this respect conservatism too presents a discourse of consolation, because it suggests that if American society and its families, churches, neighborhoods and voluntary associations were simply left alone by politics then the resources for a national renewal are already present, in the mores and the technologies of the American mainstream. On this view, had liberal governmentalism and Progressive social engineering not disturbed this mainstream in the first place, the society would be immeasurably better off today. To the extent that the proposed moral renewal requires a public policy, then, for most conservatives this is a policy centered around reversing liberal social policy of the past fifty years, by "restoring" authority to families, religious institutions, and neighborhoods.

But this repudiation of liberalism is simply implausible, as a matter of the historical record and as a question of current understanding. For liberal public policy is not an aberration or the result of insinuating and arrogant intellectual elites. It is the product of a century of political crisis and contestation. Conservative caricatures of liberal interventionism simply obscure the extraordinary accomplishments of liberalism—in subsidizing technological advance, expanding civil and political rights, limiting the predations of the market, offsetting economic instability, providing social security, expanding opportunities for home ownership and college education to middle class families—and just as simply obscure the democratically mobilized demands that made these accomplishments possible and indeed necessary. Liberal reform in the twentieth century was the consequence of the manifest failures of the political status quo ante. Liberalism is not without serious shortcomings; but the idea that things would be better if only liberals had left civil society alone ignores the fact that liberal reform has typically been a *response* to the manifest weaknesses and incapacities of civil society in the face of pressing and publicly intolerable difficulties, and to the demands of activists who have organized around these difficulties.

Think of the infamous Triangle Shirtwaist Company fire, or the Great Depression, or Jim Crow segregation, or the poverty described in Michael Harrington's best-selling *The Other America*, or the environmental abuse described in Rachel Carson's *The Silent Spring*. These were not, as conservative rhetoric would have it, figments of the arrogant liberal imagination. They were very real, and very pressing, social ills, that came to be experienced by many as serious problems requiring serious public attention. And it is intellectually dishonest, and morally negligent, to simply denounce liberals because they paid attention. The most honest and interesting conservative writers and activists today recognize this. As a result, their conservatism is ambivalent, tinged with suspicion that the mere "liberation" of civil society from governmental "interference" is not enough. Thus Robert L. Woodson, the founder and president of the National Center for Neighborhood Enterprise, has insisted that the debate between "governmentalism" and "antigovernmentalism" is misplaced, and that those who laud the voluntary efforts of grass roots civic initiatives fail to see that "the survival and proliferation of the seeds of these grassroots efforts will depend not only upon removing impediments they face but also providing substantial support for their work. . . . Rather than ending assistance to the neighborhoods that are most in crisis, we must rally our resources and redirect our support, channeling it through entities that have a track record of effectiveness." Woodson's challenge to conservatives is worth quoting at length: "The knowledge that grassroots activists can succeed where governmental programs have failed comes with a corresponding responsibility to support the neighborhood leaders who can effectively address their communities' problems. This is not a time for benevolent non-intervention. It is a time for concerted action through which the indigenous agents of healing can be buttressed by a bevy of resources garnered through corporate foundations, philanthropic associations, and government agencies."[7] Implicit in Woodson's comments is the recognition that civil society itself is flawed, impaired by certain effects of capitalism, in need of repair; also implicit is the recognition that some kind of proactive and genuinely public policy is currently needed.

As I argue in the chapters to follow, it was the great strength of organized liberalism in the twentieth century to recognize this, and to adopt a pragmatic attitude toward the use of public authority to regulate, and to enable, the development of a more solidaristic and democratic civil society. As John Dewey put it: "There is no more an inherent sanctity in a church, trade-union, business corporation, or family institution that there is in the state. Their value is also to be measured by the consequences [which] vary with concrete conditions; hence at one time and place a large measure of state activity may be indicated and at another time a policy of quiescence and laissez-faire. . . . There is no antecedent universal proposition which can be laid down because of which the functions of a state should be limited or should be expanded. Their scope is something to be critically and experimentally determined."[8] What has distinguished liberalism as a public philosophy has been its recognition of the public problems engendered by the complexities of our profoundly interdependent world, its insistence on the need to grapple with these problems by developing public means commensurate with them, and its responsiveness toward democratically articulated grievances in its pursuit of public solutions.

It is above all in the name of such a pragmatic orientation that the revitalization of organized liberalism presents itself as an important issue today. For the United States today confronts pressing public problems that demand some manner of public response. And, in the face of these difficulties, the conservative mantra of "private life good, public life bad" sounds badly out of key. Among these problems, the following stand out:

- **The breakdown of the conditions of economic growth that helped to sustain liberalism in the postwar period, and the profound social and economic insecurity deriving from new forms of accumulation and employment.** America's industrial base has dramatically eroded, as new forms of global investment and "flexible accumulation" have created a new, "lean and mean" economy in which relatively secure and high-paying employment for the mass of working- and middle-class Americans increasingly has given way to corporate downsizing, insecure employment, and low-wage jobs. The real wage of the average American nonsupervisory worker has for two decades been in decline; and during this period inequalities in the distribution of income and wealth have grown. The new, postindustrial economy promises great opportunity for some and an untold diversity of high-tech gadgets and consumer goods for mass consumption; but it also promises profound social and economic insecurity, as more and more Americans worry about their jobs, their health care, their mortgages, their consumer debt, their ability to pay for their childrens' college educations, and their own retirement. These anxieties are economic, but only partly so; for they relate to even deeper, existential questions about the meaning of a career, the character of familial obligations, and the quality of life in a fast-paced, constantly changing society.[9] These are public problems that affect vast numbers of people and that implicate the basic structure of the political economy. And any serious attempt to grapple with them would seem to require some form of serious public debate and public action that has heretofore been lacking.
- **Severe urban decay and impoverishment.** Partly as a consequence of the deindustrialization mentioned above, partly as an effect of the extraordinary suburbanization of American society in the past half century, America's inner cities are the site of intolerably high levels of unemployment, poverty, malnutrition, infant mortality, and social despair. As William J. Wilson has documented in numerous books, in the past thirty years a "new urban poverty" has developed in which unemployment, crime, family dissolution, and economic dependence combine to reinforce poverty and despair for the denizens of inner-city ghettos. He cites as typical the description of the Woodlawn neighborhood on the South Side of Chicago:

The once lively streets . . . now have the appearance of an empty, bombed-out war zone. The commercial strip has been reduced to a long tunnel of charred stores, vacant lots littered with broken glass and garbage, and dilapidated buildings left to rot in the shadow of the elevated train line. At the corner of Sixty-third Street and Cottage Grove Avenue, the handful of remaining establishments that struggle to survive are huddled behind wrought-iron bars. . . . The only enterprises that seem to be thriving are liquor stores and currency exchanges, these 'banks of the poor,' where one can cash checks, pay bills and buy money orders for a fee.[10]

That these ghettos tend to be racially segregated only exacerbates the sense that the 1967 Kerner Commission's nightmare vision of "two nations, separate but unequal," is currently being realized in American cities. A shocking 22 percent—more than one out of every five—of America's children currently live below the poverty line. Among Latinos this rate is 41 percent, and among African American children 46 percent—almost one out of every two children! Poor children are more than twice as likely as other children to suffer from undernourishment, iron deficiency, stunted growth, severe physical or mental disabilities, and severe asthma; and more than twice as likely to never finish high school. As a consequence of these and other deprivations, such children face truly dismal economic prospects. In the central cities of the United States, the unemployment rate among African Americans age sixteen to sixty is approximately 60 percent; in the suburban rings, it is still 33 percent. While well over a third of African Americans in this age group lack the experience of regular employment, almost a third of young African Americans age twenty to twenty-nine are under some kind of correctional control (incarceration in prison, probation, or parole).[11]

Indeed, the anecdotal evidence regarding the devastating effects of urban poverty is even more powerful than the abundant statistical and social scientific literature. Books such a Jonathan Kozol's *Amazing Grace: The Lives of Children and the Conscience of a Nation*, Alex Kotlowitz's *There Are No Children Here: The Story of Two Boys Growing Up in the Other America*, and Earl Shorriss's *New American Blues: A Journey Through Poverty to Democracy*,[12] vividly document the insecurity, violence, and despair that plagues inner-city neighborhoods. Perhaps the most powerful of these books is Kozol's *Savage Inequalities: Children in America's Schools*, which offers a bracing account of the physical, moral, and pedagogical decay of inner-city schools, and of the extraordinary disparities in funding, resources, and educational quality between such schools and their suburban counterparts.[13] Kozol takes us on a tour of East St. Louis, Illinois, the South Side of Chicago, the South Bronx in New York, Camden, New Jersey, Washington, D.C., and San Antonio, Texas, and he introduces us to frightened and undereducated children, demoralized and cynical teachers and school administrators, unstaffed, ill-equipped, and overcrowded classrooms, and decaying and polluted buildings that are hazardous to the children and educators who occupy them. Kozol quotes extensively from these educators, who repeatedly refer to "landscapes of hopelessness" and "the overwhelming sensation of emptiness."

In many ways American society at the dawn of the next century is characterized by a kind of de facto apartheid, or what Michael Lind has called the Brazilianization of America, "symbolized by the increasing withdrawal of the white American overclass into its own barricaded nation-within-a-nation, a world of private neighborhoods, private schools, private police, private health care, and even private roads, walled off from the spreading squalor beyond. Like a Latin American oligarchy, the rich and well-connected members of the overclass can flourish in a decadent America with Third World levels of inequality and crime."[14] Such a description may be somewhat exaggerated, but only somewhat. For the bottom quarter of our society lives under conditions that manifestly do put the lie to any meaningful conception of freedom or equality. This is a problem for the poor, but not only for them. For the new conditions of economic insecurity threaten to engulf many more Americans—especially single or divorced women and their children—within poverty. And the deterioration of inner-city life affects the quality of life of all of those who live in cities, and in so doing it diminishes the intellectual and cultural vitality of the nation as a whole. These are no trifling matters. And yet, again, they have received virtually no serious attention in the party-political debates and campaigns that capture the attention of the American public.

- **Environmental regulation and the disposal of hazardous wastes**. There can be no doubt that in the area of environmental protection enormous gains have been made in the past quarter century. The Clean Air Act, the Clean Water Act, the Endangered Species Act, the Superfund Act, and the Environmental Protection Agency itself are the results of this progress, which was very much energized by the emergence of numerous environmental organizations that coalesced into a serious political movement. There exists today an environmental consciousness that simply did not exist in the past. Al Gore Jr.'s celebrity as an "environmentalist" and author of the book *The Earth in the Balance* is merely one sign of this; while in this age of partisan bickering no aspect of a politician's persona is off limits, even Gore's opponents feel obliged to show respect for his love of the earth. Environmentalism has become as American as apple pie.

And that's the problem. For the simple fact is that the gains that have undoubtedly been achieved represent no more than a drop in the bucket of what is required to publicly address the nation's ecological ills (and its responsibility for the ecological ills of the world). This is in part a question of cleaning up the environmental damage caused by over one hundred years of industrialism and fifty years of Cold War weapons production and war preparation. The United States annually produces over 250 million metric tons of hazardous waste. According to the EPA., there exist hundreds of thousands of hazardous waste sites spread out across the country. There exist well over one thousand Superfund sites remaining to be cleaned.[15] In addition there is the growing problem of disposing of nuclear waste generated by nuclear power plants and of disposing of the prodigious chemical and nuclear wastes produced as a result of American arms production. These are serious issues, demanding public attention and significant public resources at a time of a diminished public commitment of resources. These issues currently are being played out in numerous ways: legislative controversies over the planned federal repository for nuclear waste at Yucca Mountain, Nevada, which will involve the interstate shipment of highly radioactive nuclear wastes from forty-three states; scandals involving Army Corps of Engineers cleanups of irradiated former weapons facilities; disputes over toxic waste siting and reduction in communities across the country; and heated controversies over environmental racism.[16] In spite of the lip service conventionally paid by politicians to environmental concerns, these issues percolate largely beneath the surface of political controversy and off of the radar screen of the national media. Yet they give no signs of receding from the scene. Indeed, if anything, the less they are attended to the more they will grow in consequence. For, as fellow baby boomers will no doubt attest, it's not nice to fool mother nature.

- **Political identity in a globalizing age**. At the dawn of a new century it is less clear than ever exactly what it means to be an "American." During the Cold War a certain conception of American political identity became prominent. This conception involved middle-class dreams of home ownership, economic advancement, and consumerism; a stable nuclear family based on a patriarchal "breadwinner ethic"; and staunchly patriotic support of a Cold War foreign policy in which the United States cast itself as a beacon of freedom in a world threatened everywhere by Communism.[17] As has widely been remarked, this worldview broke down in the 1960s. But its breakdown did not mean its disappearance. For this image of America persisted for those members of the so-called silent majority—epitomized by the iconic Archie Bunker—first targeted by Richard Nixon and then ridden to political power by Ronald Reagan. Contemporary American conservatism was forged out of a counterrevolution against the 1960s assault on Cold War Americanism; and the incredible appeal of films such as Steven Spielberg's *Saving Private Ryan* and books such as Stephen Ambrose's *Citizen Soldiers* and *The Victors* and Tom Brokaw's *The Greatest Generation* indicate that this cultural self-image remains powerful even today.[18]

But it is also increasingly anachronistic in our multicultural and global age. In a world of instantaneous currency flows, capital mobility, and unending flows of refugees and migrants, borders have become increasingly porous. At the same time the demographic profile of America is shifting. In the words of Todd Gitlin, we are currently experiencing "the coloring of America"; Hispanics and Asians comprise an increasingly large proportion of the population, and an even larger proportion of America's major cities. White Americans are a minority in New York, Atlanta, Chicago, Detroit, and Los Angeles.[19] What has come to be known as "multiculturalism," however, is much more than a matter of numbers. It involves a widespread preoccupation with the very question of identity, as previously marginalized groups—ethnic and racial minorities, women, gays and lesbians—have come to acquire new senses of group identity and belonging and have challenged the hegemony of the white male breadwinner ethic that had long predominated in American society. As a result, in the past three decades American political culture has become fractured along racial lines and riven by intense "culture wars" that have badly damaged the social consensus on which postwar liberalism rested. And these fractures have helped to fuel reactions on the part of politicized Christian fundamentalists and aggrieved white blue-collar workers; indeed, they have also stimulated the emergence of a potent, if small, movement of right-wing extremists.[20]

This fracturing of identity is a complex and much-discussed phenomenon. I return to it below. What I want to emphasize here is simply that there is currently great confusion and anxiety about the meaning of American nationhood and American citizenship. This confusion relates to pressing matters of domestic policy—multicultural curricula, the status of English and the role of bilingual education, civil rights for nonheterosexuals, immigration policy, affirmative action—that have proven extremely divisive and intractable.

At the same time, the challenges of the new post-Cold War world of globalization present similar questions about America's place in the world. The Cold War mentality still survives, in the Pentagon's doctrine of "rogue states," in continued American support of so-called drug war counterinsurgencies in Columbia and Peru, and in the apparent party-political consensus about the importance of some version of the "star wars" strategic missile defense system.[21] But this mentality coexists uneasily with a new liberal internationalism centered not on anticommunism but on a conception of global human rights and global free trade. This internationalism has thus far been clearest in its economic and technological dimensions; while certain foreign policy decisions, like the Kosovo war, have been justified on human rights and humanitarian grounds, there has of yet been little clear development of a global *political* agenda to replace America's Cold War commitments, something bemoaned weekly by the editors of the *New Republic*. But it is clear that the Cold War is over, however much many politicians and probably many ordinary citizens would wish it were not, and in its wake America has lost a clear sense of political purpose and a firm anchoring of political identity. In the brave new world we can no longer take our bearings from our opposition to Communism, nor can we take it from any secure sense of racial, cultural, or economic identity. What it means to be an American is thus very much in doubt.

These are pressing issues. The overused language of "legitimacy crisis" is misleading, for it mistakenly implies the likelihood of some cataclysm or point of rupture beyond which present tensions and uncertainties cannot be contained. While there is no telling the future, it is not likely that anything remotely resembling socioeconomic collapse or revolutionary upheaval is in the cards. To call these issues pressing is not to claim that their resolution is imminent or that a failure to resolve them is likely to be catastrophic. It is simply, but crucially, to call attention to deep sources of difficulty and dissatisfaction built into our current institutional arrangements. The failure to address them is likely to reproduce a social and cultural situation that is experienced by many as troubling and anxiety-producing, and is likely as well to produce further political alienation and resentment. If such issues cannot be publicly debated and addressed, then, while the political system is not doomed to collapse, it is hard to see how it can retain any meaningful sense of democratic legitimacy. Indeed, the widespread current commentary on "the disappearance of civic America" attests to this very problem.

A PROGRESSIVE REVIVAL?

The malaise of liberalism, then, is a serious problem confronting us today. Indeed, as a growing chorus of liberals have emphasized, in many ways the current impasse of liberalism mirrors the crisis from which the current form of liberalism first emerged at the dawn of the nineteenth century. Our current moment, it has been argued, is much like the Progressive era, and liberals need to revive a "progressive" politics that is modelled heavily on the Progressive politics of the last century. Just as the America of the 1890s was poised before a new century so, it is argued, are we poised at the dawn of a new century, confronting new technological opportunities and severe social challenges that demand a new spirit of progressive reform. Overwhelmed by our own interdependencies, we need new forms of social intelligence and social planning. Debilitated by an inflationary "rights revolution," we need a more pragmatic yet vigorous approach to governmental regulation. Beset by fragmentation and division, we need a new "activist public policy," centered around the problems of a postindustrial economy and the decline of middle-class living standards, that might repair the social fabric and restore "direction and coherence to national life." We must do this, neoprogressives maintain, because the only alternative is to submit to the forces of reaction, to squander the prospects for progress presented by new opportunities, and to resign our politics to a prolonged period of suffering, resentment, and antagonism.

This neoprogressivism has many sources, and incorporates a range of tactical, strategic, and ideological perspectives—party intellectuals and consultants, such as Stanley Greenberg and Robert Reich, are focused on the electoral resurgence of the Democrats; journalists and social scientists, such as E. J. Dionne Jr., Michael Lind, Theda Skocpol, William J. Wilson, and John Judis, are interested in arresting the deterioration of public policy and public civility and promoting a coherent middle-class agenda that speaks to the needs of ordinary Americans; political theorists, such as Michael Sandel, Eldon Eisenach, and Robert Putnam, are focused on the revitalization of a robust philosophy of public life; and democratic socialists, such as Joel Rogers, raise the prospect of a third party and seek to advance a long-term strategy—an updated version of Gramscian hegemony—to transform American capitalism in a more social democratic direction. These differences of emphasis do not belie an overriding commonality among these writers and activists. Most of them identify themselves as liberals; all of them take their bearing from turn of the century Progressivism, and all articulate neoprogressive themes.

There can be no doubt that this resurgent progressivism was initially stirred in large part by the devastating results of the 1994 elections, which dealt a harsh blow to Democratic strategists and to whatever hopes had remained of "New Democratic" reforms of health, education, or welfare policy. Did 1994 represent a deep realignment of the electorate and the party system, a veritable Republican Revolution, as Republican pundits have claimed ever since? Writing in the immediate aftermath of the elections, Stanley Greenberg argued that the answer was an emphatic no. There was no doubt, he admitted, that the electorate was deeply dissatisfied with politics as usual, and that this dissatisfaction was taken out on incumbent Democrats and the "big government" policies with which many were identified. Yet, Greenberg argued, most Americans do not support a wholesale assault on the welfare state, and they crave a more middle-class-oriented politics.[22] Greenberg insisted that the electorate had not shifted rightward, and indeed that large portions of the electorate remain dissatisfied by conservative Republicanism. "What is uncertain," he maintained, "is whether Democrats and progressive organizations can mobilize popular opposition to this reign of conservative Republicanism. If they can give voice to the skepticism and offer something better, this volatile electorate is ready to shift loyalty once again. If they fail, we will see a deepening disaffection with government and politics, and not merely a surge of conservatism." This is the central theme of Greenberg's book *Middle-Class Dreams*—that to restore its political credibility "the Democrats will have to engage in a profound renewal of the bottom-up idea . . . to forge a modern, middle-class-centered bottom-up party; a broad-based party encompassing the needs of the disadvantaged and working Americans and focusing on the values and interests of the middle-class."[23]

In recent years this has been a common refrain among those concerned about both the future of the Democrats and the future of left liberalism. Thus John Judis has emphasized "the importance of using economic issues to revive the class basis of the Democratic party." Liberal Democrat Paul Wellstone, Senator from Minnesota, has proposed that "a strong, progressive populist politics is in order. Progressive forces need to galvanize around, rally around, a strong opposition that offers alternatives that make a difference to ordinary people." And Vic Fingerhut, an influential Democratic political consultant, has maintained that: "The Republicans are framing everything very cleverly. They are stirring working and middle-income people against minorities, immigrants, and welfare mothers. American politics comes down to this: if working and middle-income people can be conned by Republicans into thinking that this is a fight against the undeserving poor, then the Republicans can win. But the Democrats can win if they focus attention on those elements that favor the rich and the irresponsible corporations and do not favor the working and middle-income people."[24]

Jeff Faux has similarly argued that the Democratic party has become too timid and too tied to a narrow legislative agenda, leaving its core constituencies to fend for themselves. "A liberal strategy for rebuilding the Democratic Party," he writes, "must begin with an understanding that the decline in real wages and living standards is at the heart of the anger and frustration being felt by the middle class." Democrats thus need to begin "a new conversation with the majority of Americans who work for a living. . . . They have to be willing to name and attack their enemies. . . . Exposed and unsheltered, the core constituencies of the part must regroup, reorganize, and pursue a disciplined, independent path that uses the next election to revitalize themselves as a political force." His 1996 book, *The Party's Not Over: A New Vision for the Democrats*, outlines just such a strategy.[25] In a series of essays and books Ruy Teixeira and Joel Rogers have developed a similar view: "Whatever the reasons for its current timidity, unless the Democratic Party embraces an alternative story and shows a broader willingness to contest business interests and encourage mobilization along class lines, Democrats will continue to be on the defensive and Republicans will continue to have the high ground."[26] Their recently published *America's Forgotten Majority: Why the White Working Class Still Matters*—an excerpt of which was featured in the *Atlantic Monthly*—argues that there exists a majoritarian constituency centered around class issues that is waiting to be tapped by an organized political force. On their view the failure of this constituency to be tapped is symptomatic of deficiencies not in the demand but in the supply side of American politics. And their book represents the most sustained argument yet in support of the claim that a new political majority awaits construction, and that beneath the political surface the promise of significant sociopolitical change exists.[27]

Such discussions, however, go far beyond electoral commentary, and converge with a broader and more extensive literature endorsing the revival of the project of social reform initiated by the turn-of-the-century Progressives. John Judis and Michael Lind's manifesto "For a New American Nationalism," the centerpiece of a March 1995 issue of *The New Republic*, helped to bring this broader argument to the foreground of discussion. Criticizing the incoherence of the Clinton administration and the "primitive anti-statism" of Gingrichite Republicanism, Judis and Lind called for a "new nationalism," inspired by the examples of Alexander Hamilton, Abraham Lincoln, and Theodore Roosevelt, and summed up in Herbert Croly's influential *The Promise of American Life* (1909). As they wrote:

> America today faces a situation roughly analogous to the one Roosevelt and the progressives faced. Workers are not threatening to man the barricades against capitalists, but society it divided into mutually hostile camps . . . the goal of a new nationalism today is to forestall these looming divisions in American society. . . . Can we meet these challenges? In the decades between Lincoln and Theodore Roosevelt, the country floundered as badly as it has during the last few decades. Their mountebanks were no different from ours;

their corruption was even more pervasive; and their sense of political paralysis even more profound. Still, they were able to think and act anew. As we prepare to enter the next century, we believe that we are on the verge of a similar era of national renewal.[28]

This theme is echoed in E. J. Dionne Jr.'s much-cited and extensively excerpted book *They Only Look Dead*, whose subtitle aptly sums up its argument: "Why Progressives Will Dominate the Next Political Era." Opening with an epigraph from Theodore Roosevelt, Dionne endorses a "New Progressivism," inspired by Croly, whose "task is to restore the legitimacy of public life by renewing the effectiveness of government and reforming the workings of politics." Alan Brinkley's prognosis mirrors Dionne's almost verbatim: "Liberals now need to make the case, in an inhospitable climate, that government is not intrinsically bad. They must show that it can and must play an ameliorative role in social and economic life. . . . They must be able to demonstrate that institutions of government are capable of performing their functions effectively and, equally important, that they are capable of continually 'reinventing' themselves in response to the changing world around them." Similar sentiments have been sounded by Jacob Weisberg in his book *In Defense of Government*. Reviving liberalism, he writes,

> is not a matter of starting from scratch but rather of recovering and renewing lost principles. . . . In its original incarnation, progressivism offers a needed corrective to liberalism as it has come to be defined by the Democratic Party over the past few decades. Looking back to the old Progressives, we find a liberalism without a century's accretion of bad habits, without mawkishness or excess. We find a practical, democratic approach to bettering the country. By reviving progressive ideas, liberals can fit themselves for governing again. By resurrecting the term, we can indicate a break with our recent past and our link to an older tradition.[29]

Similar prescriptions are also developed in Theda Skocpol and Stanley Greenberg's *The New Majority: Toward a Popular Progressive Politics*, an impressive collection of fourteen essays by prominent liberal intellectuals that charts an agenda for a "popular progressive politics." Like the above-mentioned texts, this one maintains that the current moment, in spite of and indeed because of its serious challenges, represents "a period of opportunity for progressives," and that while the tactical strength of liberalism is minimal, the larger unfolding social changes offer political openings for the revival of progressive liberalism.[30]

Perhaps the most ambitious of recent calls for a revival of Progressivism is Michael Lind's *The Next American Nation*. Lind proposes nothing less than a periodization of the entire sweep of American history, in which we currently stand poised for economic and cultural renewal at the dawn of a

"Fourth American Revolution." Lind proceeds from the impasse of post-sixties liberalism. Like most of the other neoprogressives cited earlier, he views this impasse as the result of two reinforcing processes—the domination of American politics by a financial and economic elite and the cultural and especially racial polarization that has helped to secure this elite domination by fragmenting the traditional constituencies of liberal democratic—and Democratic—governance and abetting the rise of the New Right. Lind's solution is a new "liberal nationalism" inspired by Hamilton and Roosevelt, that pragmatically yet vigorously deploys the powers of the federal government in "an egalitarian assault on the unjust and inequitable political institutions" of American society. Such an assault will require "a genuine democratization of our money-dominated political system and a commitment to the kind of social-democratic reforms" supported by the New Deal alliance before its demise under the weight of inflationary racial and cultural demands.

Lind's book outlines an elaborate set of social and economic policies designed to turn back the deterioration in middle-class living standards and to cement a strong reformist political coalition. Lind supports substantial campaign finance reform; a pragmatic and flexible trade policy to replace indiscriminate free trade, based on a social tariff that discriminates against low-wage foreign labor; immigration reform; more progressive taxation; an industrial policy promoting high-wage, technology-intensive growth based upon tight labor markets; and strong, national reform of health care, education, and welfare designed simultaneously to promote greater equity and efficiency. Such policies, he avers, can only succeed as part of a "war on oligarchy," which seeks to make the accumulation of private wealth compatible with overall national interests. This is an ambitious policy agenda. It is linked to an even more ambitious program of national renewal. Lind proposes nothing less than a virtual cultural revolution in American society, whereby Americans come to see themselves as part of a "trans-racial" nation committed to social justice, and the polarities of identity politics give way before a new, integral sense of American national identity centered around "middle class dreams."[31]

There are striking parallels between these reappropriations of liberal Progressivism and arguments farther to the left about the need to revive class politics in America. Indeed, the rehabilitation of Croly among liberals has been mirrored by the revival of an almost Gramscian project of developing an emergent "progressive" hegemony. Thus Michael Kazin suggested a few years back in the *New York Times* that "not since the Depression have conditions deemed so ripe for a true class-based liberal movement. Real wages have fallen over the last two decades, while income inequality has risen sharply. Employers shift manufacturing jobs to whichever country offers the cheapest labor, and unions are too weak to stop them. Meanwhile, corporate lobbyists help the Republican Congress draft bills that jeopardize occupational health and safety rules and cut back the earned-income tax credit for low-paid workers." We need, Kazin averred, a revival of "class warfare," which might move debate to the left, and raise the level of pressure for serious reforms, just as earlier movements, like the Populists and the Socialists, were able to accomplish.[32] Sidney Plotkin and William E. Scheurmann similarly suggest that "perhaps the power elite's very indifference has created a strategic opening, a systematic vulnerability to a politics of democratic change. Perhaps mainstream politics has created a gap in responsiveness to concrete problems faced by most people in their everyday lives that action from below can yet fill." They thus urge working people to "find ways to channel their anger across the divide of sectarian identities and diverse movements," and to identify with a broad, "national majority" that might institute meaningful social and economic reform.[33]

The most ambitious of these arguments has been advanced by Joel Rogers in a number of essays written in support of the New Party, a grassroots, left-wing partisan alternative to the Democrats that has enjoyed some success running local candidates in Madison, Wisconsin, Missoula, Montana, and elsewhere. Like Lind, Dionne, Skocpol, et al., Rogers sees the Democratic party as hopelessly entrenched and captive to special interests. Like Lind, he believes that American politics need a powerful counterweight to conservative Republicanism and thinks that this can only come from a reenergized left. Yet Rogers distances himself from liberalism, claiming that liberalism is too technocratic, too suspicious of mass movements, too compromised by its reluctance vigorously to challenge capitalism: "Without organized popular support, liberals cannot do the heavy lifting against entrenched and resourceful corporate actors required to enact desired policies. And without the monitoring, enforcement, and trust-inducing capacities of socially-rooted organizations, they commonly cannot administer those policies effectively." Rogers mirrors Lind in his insistence that the renewal of American democracy requires that the "social control of the economy" must be put "back on the table of American politics." But his argument is even more ambitious, for it seeks to project a coherent and reformist national agenda based on an organized mass movement "challenging corporate power and mobilizing outside the state."[34]

In Gramscian fashion, Rogers argues that this can only occur if the left proves itself capable of "uniting the particular with the universal," and that such an integration is a matter of political strategy. In this light Rogers has proposed a three-pronged strategy: (1) Democracy Now, a movement for citizen, worker, consumer, and taxpayer bills of rights designed to build on the pervasive alienation from American politics and to aid the formation of progressive organizations; (2) Sustainable America, a high-wage industrial strategy, much like Lind's, based on a social tariff, full employment, and a shortened work week; (3) The New Party, "a natural electoral vehicle for a more consolidated progressive movement—a movement that itself should be built in part through greater national coordination and presence, and in larger part, in terms of organizational strategy, from the ground up."[35]

Rogers recognizes how difficult such a political project is to achieve, how many obstacles such a revitalized left confronts. Yet he nonetheless endorses an optimism of the will, a concerted strategy designed to surmount these obstacles. "A modern Left (even more than the Left of old)," he writes, "needs to make investments in organizational infrastructure to facilitate its own coordination and impact." By the proper development of strategies, and the proper deployment of resources, a coordinated left, it is argued, can arrest the deterioration of American democracy and project a genuinely forward-looking, progressive vision of the future.[36]

Rogers's argument is not identical to the one presented by Lind, Judis, Dionne, and Greenberg. He is more critical of capitalism, more critical of the Democratic party, and also more attuned to the importance of grassroots movement building to the left of the Democrats. But there is nonetheless a striking convergence on a number of themes: that progressive liberalism is in crisis; that the so-called New Deal coalition of the "vital center" has been shattered; that the social democratic reforms of the postwar period supported by this coalition are under siege by an ideologically ascendant conservatism that has infected liberalism itself; that the only way to defend a reformist social policy and effectively to address the social and economic problems plaguing American society is aggressively to rebuild a coherent left-liberal movement, either through the Democratic party or through the creation of a third party alternative; and that the public demand for such a left-liberal movement currently exists, waiting to be articulated by ambitious policy intellectuals and tapped by resourceful and dedicated organizers.

Even more striking is the evocation of a set of historical themes closely linked with the Progressive era—the need to create a new hegemonic project, to unite the particular and the universal, to ambitiously confront and redress the destabilizing social and economic changes currently underway, to favor, in the words of Walter Lippmann, mastery over drift. In maintaining that "building a workable public activism is not a matter of starting from scratch but rather of recovering and renewing lost principles," Jacob Weisberg articulates a sentiment widely shared among these writers. Similar sentiments have been expressed by a number of academic political theorists interested in moving beyond the current liberal impasse. Thus Michael Sandel, in his *Democracy's Discontent: America in Search of a Public Philosophy*, calls for the revival of a "formative project" of cultivating civic virtue that he associates with Progressivism. Eldon Eisenach, in *The Lost Promise of Progressivism*, links the recovery of Progressive political theory to a broader public project of reclaiming America's historic memory. "To understand what Progressive academics and intellectuals have taught us," he writes, "is to understand features of ourselves and our vocations that often are unacknowledged or suppressed." Peter Levine, in *The New Progressive Era: Toward a Fair and Deliberative Democracy*, endorses political reform and a deliberative ethos reminiscent of LaFollette Progressivism. And Robert Putnam, in his *Bowling Alone: The Collapse and Revival of American Community*, appeals to the "practical civic enthusiasm" and associational tendencies of the Progressive era, recalling them as sources of inspiration, enlightenment, and instruction.[37]

This recourse to the Progressive era among so many writers and commentators is remarkable, prompting John Judis to suggest that we are now all Progressives.[38] The Progressive revival no doubt has many sources. To some extent it can be attributed to a certain nostalgia that attends the passing of a century and indeed a millennium. But even more important is the existential confusion that truly confronts liberalism today. For in many ways our moment *is* like the moment that gave rise to Progressivism, in the severity of the challenges confronting us, and in the widely perceived bankruptcy of the received wisdom about how best to confront such challenges. The appeal to Progressivism makes perfect sense. It is an understandable and indeed to a large extent justifiable temptation. But it is also mistaken.

The aspiration to revive or to revitalize Progressivism, to draw strength from its example and, in the words of Judis, to "complete its project," rests on two mistaken assumptions. The first is that such a revival is possible. The second is that such a revival is desirable. Most of this book focuses on the question of historical possibility. On the whole I find the prospect of a revitalized, organized liberalism inspired by a Progressive vision unobjectionable and indeed appealing. The policies most often supported by neoprogressives—labor law reform, a reduced work week, health care reform, solidaristic public provision, a social tariff, enhanced and targeted public investment, strong public supports for third sector social service initiatives—are attractive ones. While they would not resolve all of the problems confronting American society, they surely would help to address numerous pressing problems, and to remedy injustices that still plague American society. The idea of unifying diverse constituencies—the women's movement, racial minorities, environmentalists, community organizations, the labor movement—around such a program of social reform is equally appealing. And it is probably true that only such a progressive movement could support a meaningful program of social reform commensurate to the economic, environmental, and cultural challenges of the new century. The problem with the new progressivism is not principally its desirability but its *practicality*. The reforms, and the movement-building strategies to which they are integrally connected are, quite simply, in many ways anachronistic. They constitute an effort to revive a politics—a politics of a unified "left"—under conditions when this politics is no longer symbolically compelling or politically feasible.

The matter of political feasibility is the central concern of this book, and it is admittedly a profoundly murky one. As Albert Hirschmann has demonstrated in his book *The Rhetoric of Reaction*, ever since the Enlightenment a consistent refrain of conservative thinkers has been that meaningful social change is either futile, perverse, or horrendous.[39] It is easy to declaim about the impossibility of large-scale reform. But the problem is that time and again such declamations have proven *themselves* to be perverse. For clearly there is no necessity behind existing states of affairs. And, just as clearly, what is politically feasible can often only be ascertained after the fact. For this reason it is impossible simply to dismiss Progressive aspirations. Furthermore such aspirations, even if historically mistaken, may well be productive, inspiring worthy political efforts, generating beneficial results even when they are not wholly realized.

Yet it is the central thesis of this book that such aspirations *are* misplaced and that the conditions of social and political life today do not offer fertile soil for a Progressive revival. And, in the spirit of pragmatism earlier alluded to, if a Progressive revival is impractical, this must impair its desirability as well. For, truth be told, while Progressive aspirations are both heroic and appealing, and while they are superior to the numerous versions of laissez-faire individualism, technological determinism, pastoral nostalgia, and outright xenophobic racism that stand against them, the challenges confronting Progressivism today are not simply practical but ethical as well. To be blunt: Progressivism has always been relentlessly modernistic and technocratic. It has always been enthusiastic about human power, and it has always been enthusiastic about the beneficence of the power of the liberal state. But such enthusiasms can no longer be credulously indulged. They lack credibility both intellectually and politically. Our world today is too pluralistic, too fractious, too recalcitrant to a hegemonic project organized around a narrative of "progress" against "tradition" or "justice" against "injustice." The sources of our division are diverse; the sources of our problems are even more diverse. The challenge before us, then, is to come to terms with the historicity of Progressivism, and then to rethink the ethos and the politics best suited to realizing its genuinely liberal and humanistic aspirations for social improvement and satisfying democratic citizenship. Such a coming to terms is the goal of this book. In what follows I explore the genuine and original appeal of Progressivism, turn to a consideration of the ways in which the world has rendered it anachronistic, and finally consider in greater detail the specious reasoning behind current efforts to revive it. Having done so I turn, in the final chapter, to a discussion of the most compelling ways forward, toward practical and democratic responses to the political impasse of our times.

NOTES

1. This enthusiasm is reflected in the popularity of books like Thomas Friedman's *The Lexus and the Olive Tree* (Free Press, 1998).

2. For the most recent version of this thesis, see Roderick P. Hart, *Campaign Talk: Why Elections Are Good for Us* (Princeton, NJ: Princeton University Press, 2000). See also Lars-Erik Nelson's critical review, "Party Going," *New York Review of Books* (August 10, 2000), pp. 12–15.

3. See Robert Samuelson, *The Good Life and Its Discontents: The American Dream in the Age of Entitlement, 1945–1995* (New York: Vintage, 1997).

4. See Charles Meier, "Democracy and Its Discontents," *Foreign Affairs*, vol. 73, no. 4 (July/August 1994), pp. 48–64.

5. See Michael Joyce, "On Self-Government," *Policy Review*, vol. 90 (July/August 1998), pp. 42–48.

6. Joyce, for example, writes of "the human devastation wrought by progressivism's program of self-liberation and management by insulated elites," p. 45.

7. Robert L. Woodson Sr., "A Challenge to Conservatives," *Commonsense*, vol. 1, no. 3 (summer 1994), pp. 23–25.

8. John Dewey, *The Public and Its Problems* (Chicago: Swallow Press, 1927), p. 74.

9. See the widely cited 1996 *New York Times* special series on corporate downsizing and its costs; the *U.S. News and World Report* cover story of December 20, 1999, bearing the headline "The Price of Prosperity: Working Harder Than Ever"; James Medoff and Andrew Harless, *The Indebted Society: Anatomy of an Ongoing Disaster* (Boston: Little, Brown and Company, 1996); Juliet Schor, *The Overspent American: Upscaling, Downshifting, and the New Consumer* (New York: Basic Books, 1998); and Richard Sennett, *The Corrosion of Character: The Personal Consequences of Work in the New Capitalism* (New York: Norton, 1998).

10. William Julius Wilson, *When Work Disappears: The World of the New Urban Poor* (New York: Knopf, 1996), p. 11.

11. These statistics can be found in the Children's Defense Fund, *The State of America's Children* (Boston: Beacon Press, 1998). See also Arloc Sherman, *Wasting America's Future: The Children's Defense Fund Report on the Costs of Child Poverty* (Boston: Beacon Press, 1994), and Randy Albelda, Nancy Folbre, and the Center for Popular Economics, *The War on the Poor: A Defense Manual* (New York: The New Press, 1996).

12. Jonathan Kozol, *Amazing Grace: The Lives of Children and the Conscience of a Nation* (New York: HarperPerennial, 1996); Alex Kotlowitz, *There Are No Children Here: The Story of Two Boys Growing Up in the Other America* (New York: Anchor Books, 1992); and Earl Shorriss, *New American Blues: A Journey Through Poverty to Democracy* (New York: W. W. Norton, 1997).

13. Jonathan Kozol, *Savage Inequalities: Children in America's Schools* (New York: HarperPerennial, 1992).

14. Michael Lind, *The Next American Nation: The New Nationalism and the Fourth American Revolution* (New York: Free Press, 1995), pp. 14, 215–16.

15. See Bruce A. Williams and Albert R. Matheny, *Democracy, Dialogue, and Environmental Disputes* (New Haven, CT: Yale University Press, 1995), p. 95.

16. See the following: Erin Dunham, "Toxic Sites Grow, Money for Cleanup Drops," *Dollars & Sense*, no. 228 (March–April 2000), p. 50; Lani Sinclair, "Hazardous Waste on the Rise," *Safety and Health*, vol. 161, no. 1 (January 2000), p. 17; Michael Grunwald, "Fallout over a Nuclear Cleanup: The Corps of Engineers is Embroiled in an Environmental and Political Mess," *Washington Post National Weekly Edition* (April 17, 2000), pp. 8–9; Suzi Parker, "Burning Controversy over Weapons Disposal," *Christian Science Monitor*, vol. 91, no. 70 (March 9, 1999), p. 3; Jillian Lloyd, "In Fight over a Toxic Landfill, Round 1 Goes to Citizens," *Christian Science Monitor*, vol. 92, no. 116 (May 8, 2000), p. 2; and Dick Russell, "Mobile Chernobyls," *E Magazine*, vol. 10, no. 2 (March–April 1999), pp. 14–17.

17. See American Social History Project, *Who Built America? Volume Two: From the Gilded Age to the Present* (New York: Pantheon, 1992), pp. 483–541, for a good overview.

18. Stephen Ambrose, *Citizen Soldiers* (New York: Touchstone Books, 1998) and *The Victors: Eisenhower and His Boys: The Men of World War II* (New York: Simon & Schuster, 1998), and Tom Brokaw, *The Greatest Generation* (New York: Random House, 1998).

19. Todd Gitlin, *The Twilight of Common Dreams: Why America Is Wracked by Culture Wars* (New York: Metropolitan Books, 1995), pp. 107–14.

20. On white working-class resentment, see Thomas Byrne Edsall and Mary D. Edsall, *Chain Reaction: The Impact of Race, Rights, and Taxes on American Politics* (New York: W. W. Norton, 1991); Kevin Phillips, *Boiling Point: Democrats, Republicans and the Decline of Middle Class Prosperity* (New York: Harper, 1993); and Thomas J. Sugrue, *The Origins of the Urban Crisis* (Princeton, NJ: Princeton University Press, 1996). On the extreme racist right, see James Coates, *Armed and Dangerous: The Rise of the Survivalist Right* (New York: Hill and Wang, 1995); Ken Stern, *A Force upon the Plain: The American Militia Movement and the Politics of Hate* (Norman: University of Oklahoma Press, 1997); and Morris Dees, *The Gathering Storm: America's Militia Threat* (New York: Harper, 1997).

21. See the symposium "Rethinking Rogue States" in *Harvard International Review*, vol. XXII, no. 2 (summer 2000), pp. 46–71.

22. Stanley B. Greenberg, "After the Republican Surge," *American Prospect*, no. 23 (fall 1995), p. 72.

23. Stanley Greenberg, *Middle-Class Dreams: The Politics and Power of the New American Majority* (New York: Times Books, 1995), p. 278.

24. See John Judis, "From Hell," *New Republic* (December 19, 1994), p. 18; Paul Wellstone and Vic Fingerhut quoted in Joel Bleifus, "Working in Opposition," *In These Times* (January 23, 1995), pp. 12–13.

25. Jeff Faux, "A New Conversation: How to Rebuild the Democratic Party," *American Prospect*, no. 21 (spring 1995), pp. 36–39, and *The Party's Not Over: A New Vision for the Democrats* (New York: Basic Books, 1996).

26. Ruy A. Teixeira and Joel Rogers, "Who Deserted the Democrats in 1994?" *American Prospect*, no. 23 (fall 1995), p. 76.

27. Ruy Teixeira and Joel Rogers, *America's Forgotten Majority: Why the White Working Class Still Matters* (New York: Basic Books, 2000), and also their "America's Forgotten Majority," *Atlantic Monthly*, vol. 285, no. 6 (June 2000), pp. 66–75.

28. John B. Judis and Michael Lind, "For a New American Nationalism," *New Republic* (March 27, 1995), p. 27.

29. E. J. Dionne Jr., *They Only Look Dead: Why Progressives Will Dominate the Next Political Era* (New York: Simon and Schuster, 1996), p. 16; Alan Brinkley, "Liberalism's Third Crisis," *American Prospect*, no. 21 (spring 1995), pp. 32–33; and Jacob Weisberg, *In Defense of Government: The Fall and Rise of Public Trust* (New York: Scribner's, 1996), p. 158. See also Michael Tomasky, *Left for Dead: The Life, Death and Possible Resurrection of Progressive Politics in America* (New York: Free Press, 1996).

30. Stanley B. Greenberg and Theda Skocpol, *The New Majority: Toward a Popular Progressive Politics* (New Haven, CT: Yale University Press, 1997).

31. Michael Lind, *The Next American Nation: The New Nationalism and the Fourth American Revolution* (New York: Free Press, 1995), pp. 301–02.

32. Michael Kazin, "The Workers' Party?" *New York Times* (October 19, 1995), op ed page, A23; see also Kazin's less sanguine prognosis in "Alternative Politics: Is a Third Party the Way Out?" *Dissent*, 43 (winter 1996), pp. 22–26. Kazin elaborates on the endurance and on the obstacles to such a class politics in his *The Populist Persuasion* (New York: Basic Books, 1994).

33. Sidney Plotkin and William E. Scheuerman, *Private Interest, Public Spending: Balanced Budget Conservatism and the Fiscal Crisis* (Boston: South End Press, 1994), pp. 227–31.

34. Joel Rogers, "How Divided Progressives Might Unite," *New Left Review*, no. 210 (March/April 1995), pp. 4–5; see also "Why America Needs a New Party," *Boston Review*, 18 (January/February 1993), pp. 1–4, and "How We Might Unite," in Greg Ruggiero and Stuart Sahulka, eds., *The New American Crisis* (New York: The New Press, 1995).

35. Rogers, "How Divided Progressives Might Unite," pp. 28–30.

36. Rogers, "How Divided Progressives Might Unite," p. 30; a similar argument was developed by Stanley Aronowitz in "The Situation of the Left in the United States," *Socialist Review*, 23 (1994), pp. 5–79. Aronowitz makes the Gramscian allusion explicit: "To our understandable 'pessimism of the intellect,' we urgently need a good dose of 'optimism of the will.' Composed while in a fascist prison, Gramsci's celebrated aphorism has never had more relevance than now," p. 75.

37. Jacob Weisberg, *In Defense of Government*, p. 158; Michael Sandel, *Democracy's Discontent: America in Search of a Public Philosophy* (Cambridge, MA: Harvard University Press, 1996); Eldon Eisenach, *The Lost Promise of Progressivism* (Lawrence, KS: University Press of Kansas, 1994); Peter Levine, *The New Progressive Era: Toward a Fair and Deliberative Democracy* (Lanham, MD: Rowman & Littlefield, 2000); and Robert Putnam, *Bowling Alone: The Collapse and Revival of American Community* (New York: Simon and Schuster, 2000).

38. John Judis, "Are We All Progressives Now?" *American Prospect*, vol. 11, no. 12 (May 8, 2000), pp. 34–39.

39. Albert O. Hirschmann, *The Rhetoric of Reaction* (Cambridge, MA: Harvard University Press, 1991).

2

✛

Why a Progressive Revival?

There is something quixotic about the recent revival of Progressive themes. Neoprogressives persist in their struggle against conservative impulses—Social Darwinism, weak and decentralized government, religious obscurantism—and on behalf of genuinely noble ideals, right-minded, forward-looking, *progressive* ideals, like scientific and technological advance, social justice, and effective government. At first glance this struggle may seem perfectly consistent with the spirit of the times—a spirit of incessant technological change and the celebration of youth, youthfulness, and novelty. We surely *seem* to be living in a newly progressive era. But on second glance the Progressive impulse seems oddly out of step with the times, which are averse to the spirit of progressive reform. We live at a time in which "the age of big government" has been declared dead, and by a self-styled Progressive of sorts; at a time in which the reformist idealism of a Roosevelt, or a Kennedy, or a Johnson is as unfamiliar and unintelligible to young people as the history of the Middle Ages; and at a time in which the very term *liberal* has become an epithet of abuse, to be avoided like the plague by any self-respecting politician. Beyond this, the rationalist faith typical of Progressivism is currently under siege, by religious fundamentalists who decry modern science and rail against the teaching of Darwinian evolution and "secular humanism" in the public schools; by adherents of varieties of "postmodern" skepticism, who question the very concepts of public reason and public good that lie at the heart of Progressivism; and by the prevailing cultural tendency toward a more bland and banal know-nothingism that well suits those Yuppies and Yuppy wannabes who are absorbed in the commerce of daily life.

These tendencies hardly betoken the rise of a new Progressive agenda. Yet the appeal to Progressivism has plausibility nonetheless. For in many ways our age is like the Progressive age, in the magnitude of its problems and in their impact on the society at large. As it did a century ago, American society today is undergoing dramatic and consequential transformations, of its economy and its demography, its cultural fabric and its political system. E. J. Dionne Jr. is correct when he notes that "our time combines social change with moral crisis, enormous economic opportunity with great economic dislocation and distress [in a way that] most closely resembles the period 1870 to 1900, which led to the Progressive Era."[1]

Like the Progressives, we are experiencing the end of an old order and the emergence of a new one whose contours can only barely be glimpsed; yet while the future cannot be foretold, it seems pretty clear that it is upon us with a vengeance, and that, like the Progressives, we face severe challenges that seem to demand a coordinated, intelligent response. How to distribute work, and to distribute the benefits of prosperity, in a postindustrial society. How to address urban decay. How to remedy decades of environmental degradation, and to promote more sustainable forms of economic growth that are community-friendly. In the face of such challenges a Progressive revival has enormous appeal. For Progressivism is more than a usable past, more than an exemplary approach to public policy or an inspirational expression of reformist idealism. Progressivism represents nothing less than the birth-period of our modern industrial civilization and of our modern ways of grappling with the problems of this civilization. The Progressive era was an era in which some of the most important innovations in America's political economy were instituted, innovations that for almost a century shaped the way we think and act about politics and society. There is no mystery as to why those not complacent about the future would turn to Progressivism.

In this chapter I explore the sources of Progressivism's appeal, treating Progressivism first as a model of public policy, second as a model of political idealism, and finally as a dynamic, originary moment that bequeathed a legacy of ideas and institutions to subsequent generations of American liberals. The appeal of Progressivism is genuine, and not to be disparaged or dismissed. There is indeed much to learn from Progressivism. And the impulse to seek inspiration and guidance from an earlier moment in which the future seemed bright and reform seemed—and was—possible is a natural and understandable impulse. Yet, as I argue, to appreciate Progressivism is also to appreciate its specific historical conditions of existence, and to appreciate the distance that separates us from those conditions. But I am running ahead of myself. For it is first necessary to understand Progressivism's accomplishments, and its appeal, before we can even begin intelligently to assess its contemporary relevance, and to appreciate its limits.

PROGRESSIVISM AS PUBLIC POLICY

The second half of the nineteenth century was the scene of the most dramatic transformation of technological, economic, and social conditions that American society has ever experienced. It was during this period that the infrastructure of a modern industrial society was created.[2] We are the heirs to this creation, which profoundly and permanently altered the cultural and political landscape and called into being both a modern society and a modern public sector. Without these developments life as we know and experience it at the dawn of the twenty-first century would be inconceivable, no less for died-in-the-wool conservatives and partisans of the New Christian Right than for liberal egalitarians and so-called secular humanists. In this sense we are *all* the heirs of the Progressive era, and indeed the heirs of the Progressives, who recognized the latent promise of their age, and sought—with remarkable if not total success—to realize this promise.

During this period America went from being an agricultural nation to a society based on industrial production, from a nation of farmers large and small to a nation of factory and office workers who doubled as the consumers of an increasingly commercialized society. Between the Civil War and the turn of the century the output of manufactured goods tripled. In but a 20-year period, for example, production jumped from 68,000 tons of finished steel in 1870 to 4.2 million tons in 1890; by 1910 over 20 million tons of steel were produced. By 1890 manufacturing income exceeded agricultural income for the first time in the history of the nation, signaling the dramatic transformation of economic life by industrialism.[3]

Coincident with the rise of a full-fledged industrial capitalist economy was the growing concentration of economic production and the ascendancy of joint-stock companies, cartels, and other legal forms of large-scale corporate ownership of productive resources. This was the era of "the trusts"—Sugar Trust, Beef Trust, Steel Trust, Oil Trust, Money Trust—which came to dominate economic life and to be the subject of increasing public concern and governmental attention. It is telling that U.S. Steel—creature of J.P. Morgan, Robber Baron par excellence and founder of what was the most powerful financial empire in the United States—was the nation's first billion-dollar corporation, consolidating 200 companies and controlling 60 percent of American steel production, just as it is telling that this icon of America's rise to industrial power in 1986 changed its name to USX, betokening its flight from steel production; in truly postmodern style, the "X" signifies the independence of this multinational corporate conglomerate from any specific reference, a more-than-linguistic maneuver with profound implications for the organization of our increasingly postindustrial, "Generation X" economy. But in 1901 such developments could hardly be foreseen, and the founding of U.S. Steel symbolized the power, and the promise, of the growing association between science, industrial technology, corporate capitalism, and mass consumerism.[4]

This was also the era of the growing professionalization of American society, a time when informal structures of occupation gave way to increasingly rule-governed systems of training, authority, and regulation based on the power to organize knowledge and to confer credentials. The American Medical Association, originally formed in 1846, was reorganized in 1901 along more professional lines, resulting in an almost tenfold increase in membership in the first decade of the twentieth century; during this time other professional associations were similarly organized, among them the American Bar Association, the American Historical Association, the American Political Science Association, the American Sociological Association, the American Economic Association, the American Statistical Association, and the American Association of University Professors. More generally, this was an era in which bureaucratic forms of expertise and administration were increasingly prevalent in all walks of life, from the professions to the schools, from civil service to the organization of the shop floor.[5]

This modernization of American life was driven by a series of important technological innovations that symbolized the tremendous power of human artifice: (1) the Bessemer process of steel conversion and the Siemens-Martin open-hearth furnace, which led to phenomenal increases in steel production and made possible innovations in steel-frame construction of offices, apartment buildings, and "skyscrapers" and the construction of steel-reinforced concrete streets, bridges, waterworks, sewers, wharves, and reservoirs; (2) electric refrigeration, which greatly enhanced the meatpacking industry, leading to the further commercialization of agriculture and the creation of a national market in foods, which was further abetted by the dramatic expansion of the railroads and the creation of transcontinental railroad lines such as the Southern Pacific, the Great Northern, and the Atcheson, Topeka, and Santa Fe lines; (3) the internal combustion engine, which led to the mass production of automobiles, which jumped from just 8,000 in 1895 to 2.5 million in 1900, and called into existence a budding system of paved roads and highways; (4) the electric engine, which led to the construction of electric trolley systems, elevated train lines ("els"), and subways, enabling the relatively rapid movement of people—producers, consumers—within and between increasingly dynamic urban areas; (5) improvements in telegraph, and the inventions of the telephone and the typewriter, which dramatically enhanced the means of national, and indeed international, communication and commerce; (6) the expansion of hydroelectric power stations fueling industries and city-dwellers; (7) the installation of electric wiring and the invention of electric irons, washing machines, toasters, stoves, vacuum cleaners, and other household appliances.[6]

America at the turn of the century was like a vast construction site in which the foundations of a modern industrial society were being laid. For most Americans today it would be impossible to imagine life without steel-based construction or reinforced concrete, refrigeration, electricity, telephones, and electric appliances; just as it would be impossible to imagine life without the complexity, interdependence, and feverishness characteristic of a thoroughly modern society. If the new technologies revolutionized production and made modernization possible, without a doubt their most important effect was their impact on the formation of great cities. The age of Progressivism was the age of rapid urbanization. New York, Buffalo, Cleveland, Pittsburgh, Detroit, Chicago, Milwaukee, Kansas City, Minneapolis—between the final decades of the nineteenth century and the opening ones of the twentieth, these cities experienced phenomenal population increases, doubling, tripling, sometimes quadrupling in size. The modern American city as we know it was a creation of this period. In many ways it crystallized the dramatic economic and technological changes taking place, serving as a new way of organizing production and consumption, transportation, and housing and, most importantly, a new way of combining vast numbers of people. Indeed the modern industrial city can be seen as the crowning technological achievement of the age, the marshalling of tremendous economic, social, and engineering capacities to construct nothing less than a new way of living for increasing numbers of Americans.

And yet if this was an age of "progress," of greatly enhanced opportunities for production and consumption, social mobility, and diverse cultural experience, it was also an age of profound difficulty, disorientation, and suffering. Progress and poverty, as Henry George put it in his famous essay of the same title, were two sides of the same coin. George, writing toward the end of the nineteenth century, captured better than anyone this paradoxical unity of opposites:

> Could a man of the last century—a Franklin or a Priestley—have seen, in a vision of the future, the steamship taking the place of the sailing vessel, the railroad train of the wagon, the reaping machine of the scythe, the threshing machine of the flail; could he have heard the throb of the engines that in obedience to human will, and for the satisfaction of human desire, exert a power greater than that of all the men and all of the beasts of burden of the

earth combined; could he have seen the forest tree transformed into finished lumber—into doors, sashes, blinds, boxes or barrels, with hardly a touch of the human hand . . . could he have conceived of the hundred thousand improvements which these only suggest, what would he have inferred as to the social condition of mankind? Out of these bounteous conditions he would have seen arising, as necessary sequences, moral conditions realizing the golden age of which mankind has always dreamed . . . [Yet] just as a community realizes the conditions which all civilized communities are striving for, and advances in the scale of material progress . . . so does poverty take a darker aspect. . . . The "tramp" comes with the locomotive, and almshouses and prisons are as surely the marks of "material progress," as are costly dwellings, rich warehouses, and magnificent churches. Upon streets lighted with gas and patrolled by uniformed policemen, beggars wait for the passer-by, and in the shadow of college, and library, and museum, are gathering the more hideous Huns and fiercer Vandals of whom Macauley prophesied.[7]

The image is a powerful one. Warehouses, mansions and cathedrals, schools, libraries, and museums—human constructions, looming high on the skyline, the symbols of wealth, refinement, and cultural enrichment— and beneath them the apparitions of the dispossessed, of beggars, and child laborers, symbols of poverty and degradation. For George progress offers the hope of human betterment and yet casts a dark and foreboding shadow; "the promised land flies before us like the mirage. The fruits of the tree of knowledge turn as we grasp them to apples of Sodom that crumble at the touch."

The new industrial city symbolized this state of affairs, presenting extraordinary new opportunities for social interaction and yet embodying a host of new and pressing social difficulties: the disposal of the prodigious amounts of garbage and sewage produced by ever-greater numbers of factories and households; the provision of reliable, fresh water supplies for the rapidly expanding population of city dwellers; the construction of paved streets, first in brick and eventually in asphalt, in order to carry the heavy traffic demanded by urban production and consumption, and by the fast pace of city living, and the provision of new forms of reliable—and affordable—public transportation; the construction of apartment buildings and tenement housing and the management of the severe problems of overcrowding and unsanitary conditions that they presented; the need for dramatically expanded police and fire services to deal with the new problems of "social coordination" and "social control" created by high urban density; and the need for new schools, and new approaches to learning, to accommodate the cultural diversity, and modernism, of city life and to incorporate the millions of rural immigrants who constituted a large part of the new urban population.

As Jane Addams described Chicago's Nineteenth Ward:

> The streets are inexpressibly dirty, the number of schools inadequate, factory legislation unenforced, the street-lighting bad, the paving miserable and altogether lacking in alleys and smaller streets, and the stables defy all laws of sanitation. . . . Hundreds of houses are unconnected with the street sewer. . . . Back tenements flourish; many houses have no water supply save the faucet in the backyard; there are no fire escapes; the garbage and ashes are placed in wooden boxes which are fastened to the street pavements.[8]

Addams's revulsion is more than physical; it is moral (and arguably moralistic). For the scene she describes evidences not simply filth and poverty but also a social disrepair and degradation that was deeply at odds with America's self-image. Like George, Addams saw that the turn-of-the-century American city was an ambiguous achievement, a symbol of both technical prowess and moral turpitude. In the *Communist Manifesto*, Karl Marx and Friedrich Engels describe the unprecedented innovation and productivity of the bourgeoisie, yet also the unanticipated and contradictory effects of such ingenuity. Bourgeois society, they write, is like "the sorcerer, who is no longer able to control the powers of the nether world whom he has called up by his spells."[9] The image of "progress" run amok weighed heavily on the minds of Progressive reformers.

They saw that the process of modernization was culturally and economically wrenching, a deracinating process only exacerbated by the periodic eruption of devastating and disorienting business cycles. The evolution of modern society in America was a process of punctuated rather than graduated evolution; and depressions, like the great Panic of 1893, vividly dramatized the new realities of full-fledged industrial capitalism and the problems of overproduction, mass unemployment, and underconsumption these realities presented. As the famous economist Joseph Schumpeter put it, a never-ending cycle of "creative destruction" constitutes the essence of modern capitalism; and at the dawn of the "second"—and more decisive—industrial revolution of the late nineteenth century, the creativity no less than the destructiveness was a source of enormous difficulty, representing great promise but also a daunting challenge.

Progressive politics was above all an effort to respond in kind to this unprecedented growth of social power, to develop and exercise a commensurate *public* power, through a robust public sector that could help to manage, and to "solve," the many "social problems" thrown up by the wholesale modernization of American life. As the historian Carl Degler has claimed, Progressivism was "a response to the challenge of the city and the factory, an attempt to bring to heel the untamed forces which had almost reduced the American Dream to a mockery."[10]

We normally associate this effort to subdue "untamed forces" with federal legislation and with national politicians, such as Theodore Roosevelt or Woodrow Wilson, and with good reason, for Progressivism spurred the development of the first truly national administrative state, and with it helped to constitute a new, thoroughly national American political identity. Yet Progressive politics was driven by urban-based reform movements and propelled by a wave of legislative reforms and public policy innovations at the state and local levels. These reforms sought to use public resources and public agencies to counter the above-mentioned problems thrown up by industrialization and urbanization and to create an environment in which American liberal and democratic ideals could be realized under new conditions.[11]

- Juvenile courts and detention centers were established to deal with problems of "juvenile delinquency."
- Public playgrounds and parks were constructed to provide "healthy" outlets for newly urbanized masses otherwise confined to factories and tenements.
- An elaborate system of public health was set up, promoting cholera diagnostic testing and diphtheria vaccination; municipal ordinances required the reporting and treatment of tuberculosis; public water supplies were purified, and chlorinated, to prevent outbreaks of disease; and baby clinics and visiting nurses were established, at public expense, to help promote the health of young children.
- State and municipal laws were passed and agencies established to regulate "public utilities"—electric power plants and lines, waterworks, "sanitation"—insurance rates, and the rates, and routes, of municipal trolley and train lines; indeed, in a number of places, most notably Wisconsin, laws were passed providing not simply for the regulation but the public ownership of such public resources.
- Pure food and drug laws were passed throughout the country.
- A range of laws, codes, and ordinances were passed providing for the municipal and state regulation of housing, establishing public standards for fire safety, requiring tenement rooms and hallways to have lighting, regulating room size, plumbing standards, building occupancy limits, requiring fire escapes and establishing comprehensive building codes.
- State laws were passed throughout the country limiting child labor and instituting school attendance requirements; regulating worker health and safety by requiring the installation of power shutoff switches in factories, the provision of adequate lighting and first-aid

stations; establishing minimum-wage and maximum-hour laws for selected classes of workers, usually public employees and women; establishing systems of worker compensation in case of injury that would both provide disability pay and limit employer liability for accidents and injuries on the job; and, in some cases, setting up primitive systems of unemployment compensation.

- Progressive tax reform was enacted in many states, seeking to expand the fiscal power of the public sector while distributing the burdens of taxation in a more "equitable" manner consistent with the idea that public-sector services are public goods.

- The practice of passing municipal zoning ordinances was invented, along with such fiscal devices as the establishment of municipal bond tax exemptions and the rationalized tax assessment of urban real estate, all designed to enhance the tax and regulatory powers of local governments so that they could more efficiently administer this new array of public responsibilities.

But perhaps the most important of these public policy innovations were the "progressive" reforms of public education, inspired by the educational writings of John Dewey, and spearheaded by the "Gary system" pioneered by William Wirt in Gary, Indiana. In the words of Randolph Bourne, progressive education sought "to treat the public school as a public service, and apply to it all those principles of scientific direction which have been perfected for the public use of railroads, telephones, parks and other 'public utilities.'"[12] Progressive educational reformers sought to reorient the practice of public education, transforming the schools from transmitters of rote knowledge and small-town moral rectitude into active promoters of the social *and* civic skills required by the newly modernizing and urbanizing society. These reformers succeeded in instituting a remarkable number of new programs and policies: vocational guidance and training, industrial education, and "shop" classes designed to acquaint young prospective factory workers with the "industrial arts"; "home economics" classes designed to prepare girls for a life of domestic labor and stewardship; special education for children with learning difficulties and special needs; school hot lunches and a heightened attention to nutrition and nutritional planning; the employment of school nurses and the regular administration of medical exams and inoculations; kindergartens and day care facilities designed to offer preschool enrichment for urban children; the establishment of middle schools and the reform of high schools as funnels for higher education and professional training; the institution of compulsory attendance laws designed to require some form of academic training for all children; the professionalization of teaching, marked by the establishment of teachers' colleges and systems of public accreditation of teachers and schools; and the municipal centralization of education, increasingly organized around Boards of Education that sought to achieve a uniform curriculum.[13] Progressive educational reform represented much more than the institution of new ways of organizing schools and transmitting knowledge; it was nothing less than an organized, rationalized project of "socialization," designed to transform the children of mostly Eastern and Southern European immigrants, as well as migrants from the American countryside itself, into *American citizens*, possessed of the requisite linguistic, technical, and social skills necessary to function in an urban, industrial, capitalist society.

This wave of municipal and state reform was paralleled at the federal level where, in the thirty years between 1890 and 1920, the foundations of the "regulatory state" were laid by a series of important pieces of national legislation: the Sherman Antitrust Act of 1890, the Pure Food and Drug Act of 1906, the Federal Reserve Act of 1913, the Sixteenth Amendment of 1913, which provided for the federal income tax, the Federal Trade Commission Act of 1914, and the Clayton Antitrust Act of 1914. These initiatives, when taken together, resulted in a dramatic enhancement of the power of the federal government in regard to trade policy, banking, health and environmental regulation, and labor law, a power underwritten by the growth of the federal bureaucracy—the establishment of the Departments of Agriculture, Interior, and Labor—and of the executive office of the President.

In one respect these federal developments represented a continuation of the municipal and state drive toward reform sweeping across the nation. Yet in another respect they represented an important departure, because they involved the thorough *nationalization* of American politics, the creation of a robust governmental power, at the level of the nation-state as a whole, charged with the responsibility, in the words of the historian Morton Keller, of "regulating a new society." Roosevelt's "New Nationalism" and Wilson's "New Freedom" converged on what political scientists have come to call a new "policy-regime" in the United States, a "regulatory state" that assumed a public responsibility for the smooth and efficient operation of an increasingly complex industrial society and that sought to defray, to absorb, and, when possible, to limit the third party costs and unintended consequences of the furious pace of social and economic activity.[14] As Elihu Root, one of Theodore Roosevelt's principal advisors, put it: "Today almost all Americans are dependent upon the action of a great number of other persons mostly unknown . . . [requiring] that great combination of all citizens which we call government to do something more than merely keep the peace—to regulate the machinery of production and distribution and safeguard it from interference so that it shall continue to work." Government, in the words of Henry Stimson, a confidant of Woodrow Wilson, could no longer be seen as "a mere organized police force, a necessary evil, but rather [as] an affirmative agency of national progress and social betterment."[15]

This new practice of government laid the foundation of American public policy in the twentieth century. The regulatory reforms of the early twentieth century; the social democratic reforms of the New Deal era; the dramatically enhanced national authority, and military power, of the American state, which underwrote American global leadership in the First World War, the Second World War, and the Cold War; the civil rights and Great Society reforms of the 1960s—these developments, which have defined American political life for over a century, would not have been possible without the transformation of the American national state that took place during the Progressive era, and that was the principal achievement of the Progressives. One could go even further. Without these political developments, the expansion of American capitalism as we know it today, first nationally and then globally, would have been inconceivable. It has become commonplace in recent years to decry the Progressive impulse, to denounce "liberalism" for its governmentalism and its "elitism," to endlessly sing the praises of Jeffersonian antistatism and of free markets. But the society that we take for granted, with its buildings, its highways real and virtual, its level of consumer abundance, its legal and political order, and above all its character as a pluralistic nation with an integrated sense of national identity, owes its existence to the changes engineered by the Progressives.

American society at the turn of the century was a society in disarray, overcome by the birth pangs of full-fledged industrialization, disoriented by the rapid urbanization of rural populations both native and immigrant, confused about the economic and political tendencies toward nationalization and powerfully wedded to long-standing traditions of localism and regionalism. Progressivism represented a largely successful effort to steer a way through these challenges, to harness them in the name of a modernizing economic and political order.

PROGRESSIVISM AS VISION

We have apparently been witnessing . . . the end of one epoch and the beginning of another. A movement of public opinion, which believes itself to be and calls itself essentially progressive, has become the dominant formative influence in American public life.

—Herbert Croly, *Progressive Democracy* (1914)

Behind the changes wrought by Progressive politics was a "movement of public opinion," a constellation of ideas, and intellectual energies, that came to have a "formative influence" in American public life. Progressivism, indeed, was much more than a new institutional arrangement or "policy regime"; it was a *hegemonic ideology*, merging a variety of intellectual currents and providing a unifying vision of social reform. An idealistic vision, its proponents believed themselves to be on the cutting edge of historical change, veritable "progressives" battling the forces of complacency and reaction. In this section I delineate the main features of progressivism as an ideology or ethos. But before doing so it is important to issue two caveats.

First, it is important to note the diversity of ideas and thinkers falling under the rubric of Progressivism. Any generalizations about Progressive social thought are bound to oversimplify, to pass over subtleties of argumentation, and to highlight certain developments at the expense of others. That is to say, they are *generalizations*, indispensable to the intellectual historian, but to be approached with a certain degree of caution nonetheless. Such caution is particularly appropriate when considering the Progressive era, because this period has been grist for the mill of so many different scholarly interpretations. For me the most important features of Progressive thought have to do with its modernist aspirations and its nationalizing impulses. The Progressivism that concerns me is what I would call mainstream Progressivism, which sought to underwrite the creation of new state regulatory powers, at the level of the city and the level of the nation-state itself. But there can be no doubt that Progressivism also had what might be called subterranean currents, more improvisational efforts to institute "progressive" social or political change by promoting new forms of citizen involvement such as social centers, tent meetings, and other modes of civic association. Kevin Mattson, for example, in his book *Creating a Democratic Public: The Struggle for Urban Participatory Democracy During the Progressive Era*,[16] makes much of these subterranean currents. As well he should, for they were important efforts, with contemporary relevance. But they were, I would argue, *subterranean*, and it is to more ambitious public policies, and not these localized and participatory initiatives, to which most current neoprogressives appeal when they argue in favor of a Progressive revival.

Second, it is important to note that there was of course no one-to-one correspondence between the vision put forth by Progressive intellectuals and the actual policies enacted by governing institutions. Progressive politics, in other words, was never a pure expression of "progressive" ideas; at every step along the way progressive ideas were shaped, directed, and deflected by a complex array of political forces.[17] But this too is a truism of politics. And having said it, it is worth noting the striking degree to which Progressive politics was informed by a coherent vision of public life and would have been inconceivable without this vision.

While the Progressive intellectuals, then, did not create a new public philosophy ex nihilo, and while Progressive public policy did not spring from the minds of these intellectuals like Athena from the forehead of Zeus, Progressive intellectuals did give expression to the changes taking place in society, and comprehended them in a manner that did profoundly shape American political thought for the rest of the century. In his *Drift and Mastery*, one of the central texts of this new Progressive ethos, Walter Lippmann put this interrelationship of theory and practice well:

> The kind of vision which will be fruitful to democratic life is one that is made out of latent promise in the actual world. There is a future contained in the trust and the union, the new status of women, and the moral texture of democracy. It is a future that can in a measure be foreseen and bent somewhat nearer to our hopes. A knowledge of it gives a sanction to our efforts, a part in a larger career, and an invaluable sense of our direction. . . . A vision of latent hope would be woven of vigorous strands; it would be concentrated on the crucial points of contemporary life, on that living zone where the present is passing into the future. It is the region where thought and action count. Too far ahead there is nothing but your dream; just behind there is nothing but your memory. But in the unfolding present man can be creative if his vision is gathered from the promise of actual things.[18]

What, then, were the main features of this vision gleaned from the "latent promise" of the world?

First, it was a forward-looking, experimental vision, in revolt against what the intellectual historian Morton White has called "formalism," whether this be the case-method of jurisprudence, the deductivism of neoclassical economics, or the narrow constitutionalism of history and political science as these disciplines were conventionally practiced. Formalistic approaches such as these were the dominant intellectual tendencies in Gilded Age America, and they tended to inhibit ambitious political thinking and social reform. As White has argued, there are striking and important affinities between John Dewey's "instrumentalism," the "legal realism" of Oliver Wendell Holmes Jr., the "institutionalism" of Thorstein Veblen, Henry Carter Adams, Richard Ely, and the "new historiography" of Charles Beard and James Harvey Robinson. As he writes, these writers were "leaders of a campaign to . . . emphasize that the life of science, economics, and law was not logic but experience in some streaming social sense. . . . All of them insist on coming to grips with life, experience, process, growth, context, function."[19]

The Progressive vision was functionalist, viewing politics, religion, culture, and property as interdependent parts of a larger, evolving whole from which they drew their meaning. On this view no social practices or institutions were sacred; everything derived its sanction from the way it fit within a broader context. And similarly, no practices or institutions were immutable; the social world, like the broader natural world in which it was embedded, was seen as dynamic and fluid, having a complex and contingent past and an equally complex and contingent future. Progressive social inquiry, then, refused to accept anything as given; it sought to develop a synthetic understanding of the totality of social life, identifying pressing problems of difficulty and adjustment, evaluating the capacity or incapacity of existing institutions to address such problems, and attempting to discern forms of deliberate change that might remedy them. The impact of Darwinism in propelling this intellectual agenda cannot be exaggerated, for Darwinism promoted a resolutely naturalistic and historicist understanding of the universe. While Darwinism is often—and rightly—viewed as having been the basis of a "social Darwinist" defense of economic laissez faire, conservatives were by no means the only Darwinists in late-nineteenth-century America, and so-called reform Darwinists equally drew upon an evolutionary view to defend the importance of social intelligence and "mutual aid" as distinctively adaptive human capacities.

Progressive social thought was thus *pragmatic*, in the general sense in which it sought to address practical concerns of politics and society, and in the specific sense in which it was heavily influenced by the genre of philosophical pragmatism whose principal innovators were William James, Charles Sanders Piece, and Dewey. In many ways pragmatism can be seen as the general self-consciousness of the Progressive age. It repudiated the sterile philosophical opposition of empiricism and idealism in favor of the view that knowledge is the product of transactions between human inquirers and the problematic world that humans inhabit. It emphasized the importance of inquiry as a disciplined and productive activity that takes its bearings from the practical problems of human living rather than from canonical religious or political texts. It supported an integrated approach to inquiry, valorizing the scientific method as a form of intellectual discipline equally appropriate to the study of nature, human individuals, and society itself. Writing in 1917 on "The Need for a Recovery in Philosophy," Dewey summed up the pragmatic impulse:

> I believe that philosophy in America will be lost between chewing a historic cud long since reduced to woody fibre, or an apologetics for lost causes . . . or a scholastic, schematic formalism, unless it can somehow bring to consciousness America's own needs and its own implicit principle of successful action. This need and this principle, I am convinced, is the necessity of a deliberate control of policies, by the method of intelligence, an intelligence which is not the faculty of intellect honored in textbooks, and neglected elsewhere, but which is the sum-total of impulses, habits, emotions, records, and discoveries which forecast what is desirable and undesirable in future possibilities, and which contrive ingeniously in behalf of imagined good.[20]

Pragmatism viewed inquiry as a form of living, relevant, deliberate adjustment to and engagement with the world.

Pragmatism was a philosophy of and for a changing world. As Dewey wrote elsewhere: "Striving to make stability of meaning prevail over the instability of events is the main task of intelligent human effort."[21] This was the impulse behind Progressivism—to arrest and to direct the flow of incessant social change, to constitute a stability of meaning, an adequate and effective understanding of rapidly unfolding events and processes, to allow men to get a "grasp" on the situation, both in the sense of an articulate comprehension and in the sense of a measure of substantial *control*. In this regard Progressive thinking was firmly within the modernist conception of political thought that can be traced from Niccolo Machiavelli, Francis Bacon, and Thomas Hobbes through the Federalists, Alexis de Tocqueville and Karl Marx, all of whom sought, in different ways, to develop a "new science of politics" to channel and redirect the flow of disruptive historical currents. As the Progressive Lippmann put it, there are but two alternatives—drift or mastery.

Such a view of "intelligent human effort" is anathema to any kind of complacency toward or reverence for the world of human affairs, for it privileges human initiative—the initiative of inquiry and the initiative of constructive social action. In place of unthinking acceptance, religiously sanctioned fatalism, or credulity about the movement of history, Progressives endorsed a vigorous extension of the critical method of modern science as a tool of inquiry and reform. As Dewey and James Tufts put it in their influential *Ethics*, published in 1908: "The need of the hour seems . . . to be the application of methods of more deliberate analysis and experiment. The extreme conservative may deprecate any scrutiny of the present order; the ardent radical may be impatient of the critical and seemingly tardy processes of the investigator; but those who have considered well the conquest which man is making of the world of nature cannot forbear the conviction that the cruder method of trial and error and the time-honored method of prejudice and partisan controversy need no longer dominate the regulation of life and society. They hope for a larger application of the scientific method to the problems of human welfare and progress."[22] In this regard Progressive social thought reiterated long-established Enlightenment themes, valorizing reason over prejudice, and critical inquiry over custom, Scripture, or common sense; but it did so in a post-Darwinian and thoroughly modernizing world.

These critical impulses were set to work in the name of a new conception of the meaning of democracy designed to satisfy the radically changed conditions of life on the eve of a new century. As Felix Frankfurter noted in a retrospective on Progressivism: "Behind the diverse and discordant movements for reform . . . lay the assumption that the traditional hopes of

American democracy had been defeated by social and economic forces not contemplated by the founders of the nation. But there was lacking a thoroughgoing critical analysis of the ways in which Americanism had become merely a formal creed."[23] In undertaking such an analysis Progressives engineered a substantial revision of the liberalism that had dominated American public discourse since the colonial period.

Modern liberalism is distinguished historically by its concern for individual liberty. Liberalism emerged in the seventeenth century in England, and flourished throughout Europe in the aftermath of the French Revolution. Its principal theorists were John Locke, the Baron Charles Secondat de Montesquieu, Adam Smith, Thomas Jefferson, James Madison, Benjamin Constant, Alexis de Tocqueville, and John Stuart Mill. Liberalism from its inception was a philosophy of *liberation*, seeking to remove the constraints on individual freedom associated with the Old Order—such constraints as feudal and later mercantile property relations, aristocratic and monarchical government, religious intolerance and persecution, and state infringements on freedom of expression, movement, and association.

By removing these constraints, classical liberals sought to liberate individuals so they might develop and express themselves as autonomous beings subject only to their own purposes. The voluntary exchanges characteristic of the so-called free market, the voluntary observances associated with religious disestablishment and "free exercise," and the voluntary political associations and allegiances typical of representative government were the central achievements of liberalism. Indeed, they constituted the principal aspirations of liberalism, from the time of Locke in the seventeenth century to the time of Mill in the nineteenth. That this liberalism is usually called "classical liberalism" underscores both its foundational and its anachronistic character.

In the latter part of the nineteenth century this "classical" liberalism became unglued by the fruits of its own success. In short, the civil freedoms achieved by classical liberalism and the dynamic economic forces unleashed by capitalist development had engendered new forms of inequality and new forms of corporate power and privilege. With the full development of industrialization, urbanization, and bureaucratization, social life became more complex, more interdependent; in the words of the twentieth-century liberal writer Bertrand Russell, modern society had entered an "age of organization." In such a setting standard liberal nostrums about individual freedom and responsibility were disrupted, for individuals now found themselves bound together in an ever-more intricate division of labor, profoundly affected by the often distant actions of anonymous and often unaccountable others. As the Progressive writer E. A. Ross put it in his influential *Sin and Society* (1907): "Modern sin takes its character from the mutualism of our time. . . . Nowadays the water main is my well, the trolley car is my carriage . . . the policeman's billy my fist. . . . I rely upon others to look after my drains, invest my savings, nurse my sick, and teach my children. . . . The modern high-power dealer of woe wears immaculate linen, carries a silk hat and a lighted cigar, sins with calm countenance and a serene soul, leagues and months from the evil he causes. . . . Modern sins are impersonal. . . . The hurt passes into that vague mass, the 'public,' and is there lost from view."[24]

In the face of these transformations in the scale and complexity of social life, those who identified with broadly liberal ideals faced a dilemma—how could the liberal values of individual independence and autonomy be realized in a social setting characterized not by independence but by extraordinary *interdependence*? How could liberalism cope with the problems thrown up by industrialization and urbanization, by the new forms of power and inequality characteristic of a highly concentrated corporate economy? And how could liberalism meaningfully assess, and regulate, social responsibility under conditions where the causes of harm are often unintended and the agents of harm are "leagues and months" removed from the consequences of their agency? The Progressives were, roughly speaking, liberals who sought seriously to address these challenges, who sought to revise liberal political thought, to rethink what individual autonomy, dignity, and responsibility might mean under the new conditions of social interdependence and feverish, impersonal change. In doing so they confronted two ideological antagonists.

On one side stood a range of egalitarian ideologies, including agrarian Populism and Debsian socialism, that supported the radical redistribution of property and the public enforcement of social rights, whether this be through public ownership of utilities, oil companies, and railroads; food and drug legislation that sought to regulate the production and sale of classes of consumer goods; workmen's compensation, and labor laws regulating occupational safety and health; public forms of credit, assistance to widows, children, and the aged, and unemployment compensation; and, in their more radical forms, the creation of new forms of collective and cooperative ownership of industrial and agricultural property to replace the capitalist system of private ownership of the means of production. As I argue in the next chapter, these demands had substantial currency during this period. They were radical both in the ends they sought and in the means typically employed by their proponents, which included the ballot box but also included strikes, sit-ins, large public demonstrations, and other forms of direct action that often precipitated violent confrontations and repressive governmental backlashes.

On the other side were more classically oriented liberals, firmly wedded to the idea that any kind of governmental action represented an infringement on individual liberty that ought to be uncompromisingly opposed. Among these the most adamant were supporters of the doctrine of "Social Darwinism," an ideology whose most famous proponent was an English writer named Herbert Spencer, and whose most prominent American supporter was the influential Yale sociologist William Graham Sumner. Social Darwinism wedded a commitment to laissez-faire economics to a version of the Darwinian idea of natural selection. According to this view, in society as in nature only the fittest can survive. Those who succeed in a capitalist society thus prove themselves by their success to be virtuous and worthy, and those who fail thereby demonstrate their vice and obvious lack of worth. It is thus both an injustice and a corruption of the social body, so to speak, for government in any way to intervene or to regulate the freedoms of the marketplace so as to limit the power of the wealthy or powerful or to assist those lacking in wealth or power. On this view each individual is responsible only to himself. If the wealthy wish to offer charity to those less well off than themselves, this— as Andrew Carnegie, Andrew Mellon, John C. Rockefeller, and other "robber baron" philanthropists made clear—is their prerogative. But justice makes no demands on them, and any limitations on their right to dispose of their property and wealth as they choose constitute infringements of fundamental liberties and indeed contraventions of nature itself.

It was amidst this ideological antagonism between classically liberal social Darwinists on the one side and radicals and socialists on the other that American Progressives sought to renovate liberalism. In pursuing this agenda they followed on the heels of British writers, such as T. H. Green and Leonard Hobhouse, who in the 1880s began to advocate a "new liberalism" for the new age. As Green put it, in his oft-cited *Liberal Legislation and Freedom of Contract*, freedom for the liberal means more than "merely freedom from restraint or compulsion . . . [but] a positive power or capacity of doing or enjoying something worth doing or enjoying . . . a power which each man exercises through the help or security given him by his fellow men."[25] Green argued that a liberal society so committed to freedom must assure the conditions under which every individual can so act. Just as we condemn slavery, he argues, and would not validate a contract whereby one is relegated to slavery, however voluntarily this contract may seem to have been entered upon, we must be prepared to limit freedom of contract *whenever* this freedom impairs the health, safety, or dignity of the individuals in question. The new liberalism was an activist liberalism, committed to what philosophers call a positive conception of liberty as a capacity for meaningful self-direction. Wherever the conditions for such autonomy were absent or denied, the new liberalism sought to provide them through governmental action. Such collective provision was justified by these liberals in terms of the need to equitably allocate the basic conditions of liberty to all individuals.[26] Liberty, they insisted, could not be meaningful if it remained the province only of the privileged.

American Progressives applied this new liberalism to the unique conditions and traditions of the United States. Progressives helped to organize new disciplines and academic departments committed to social reform. They produced a steady stream of books, monographs, studies, articles, and essays on the subject of social reform. They dominated the pages of numerous journals and magazines, and they created their own journals and magazines. Without doubt the most influential was *The New Republic*, founded in 1914 by Herbert Croly along with Walter Weyl and Walter Lippmann. By the first decade of the new century Croly had become a veritable apostle of Progressivism, and his 1909 *The Promise of American Life* presented the most comprehensive justification for the thoroughgoing reform of American political life and an equally comprehensive reconstruction of liberalism as a political philosophy.[27]

Croly writes in the tradition of Green, Hobhouse, and the "New liberalism" in En-gland, but also in the tradition of The Federalists—especially Alexander Hamilton, to whom he frequently and favorably refers in *The Promise*—and Abraham Lincoln. Like The Federalists, Croly is interested in developing a new political science that can be the basis for recreating political institutions and resolving problems of disorder; like them, and like Lincoln, Croly rejects Jeffersonian localism, and supports a robust federal government as the principal agency of such a recreation.

The basic theme of *The Promise* is that American democracy represents a promise, an ideal or potential, but like all potentials the promise of American democracy requires actualization, and needs to be fulfilled. Croly's central point is that a potential in no way guarantees its own fulfillment, and that the promise of American life is thus a *responsibility* rather than a prophetically or providentially assured result. As he writes:

> The fault in the vision of our national future possessed by the ordinary American . . . [consists in] the expectation that the familiar benefits will continue to accumulate automatically. In his mind the ideal Promise is identified with the processes and conditions which hitherto have very much simplified its fulfillment, and he fails sufficiently to realize that the conditions and processes are one thing and the ideal Promise quite another. Moreover, these underlying social and economic conditions are themselves changing, in such wise that hereafter the ideal Promise, instead of being automatically fulfilled, may well be automatically stifled.[28]

The Promise of American Life is above all a call to action. Americans, Croly argues, take freedom and prosperity for granted. They assume that these values are assured by the conditions that once brought them forth—by the institutions of local self-government, by the self-regulating processes of the economic market, by the availability of inexpensive land. At an even deeper level, Americans believe that the "destiny" of America is to be a land of the free and home of the brave, and that the circumstances of the "New World" almost providentially assure this freedom. Croly adamantly repudiates such complacency. Not only do existing conditions *not* automatically promote the promise of freedom and prosperity; they seem "automatically"—if left to work according to their own inherent tendencies—to *stifle* this promise.

Croly identifies a number of profoundly important changes that put the lie to the myth of American exceptionalism and that demand a responsible, coordinated response—the rise of new sociopolitical agents in the form of "the business specialist," i.e., corporate manager, the union movement, and the professional politician; the "end of the frontier" forewarned by Frederick Jackson Turner; and the demographic and cultural pressures caused by mass immigration. As a result, he argues, "the earlier homogeneity of American society has been impaired." This he calls "the social problem," which is not so much a problem of class inequality—though it is in part a problem of class inequality—as it is a problem of profound and unsettling social division. "In its deepest aspect," he writes, "the social problem is the problem of preventing such divisions from dissolving the society . . . of keeping such a highly differentiated society fundamentally sound and whole."

The solution to this problem, he goes on, requires "the substitution of a conscious social ideal for the earlier homogeneity of the American nation."[29] The phrase "conscious social ideal" is almost the mantra of the book. Croly appeals repeatedly to the idea of creating a "national purpose" or "national good faith" and consistently sets this project against the ideas of "non-interference" and "automatic harmony" that he associates with the worst kind of Jeffersonian primitivism. American freedom, Croly insists, requires a public policy designed actively to promote freedom. And beyond this, it requires a collective purpose, a sense of national identity that transcends all particular identities and that is capable of legitimating a regulatory state that alone can provide the conditions of freedom for ordinary Americans. In this respect Croly is a latter-day Hegel, writing in the name of a universal state based on a "conscious social ideal."

Yet whereas Hegel famously believed that "the owl of Minerva rises at dusk"—that philosophic and political wisdom is retrospective, arriving on the historical scene after the fact—Croly, Progressive that he was, insisted that public philosophy and public purpose must be proactive, anticipatory, and indeed *formative*. In this regard Croly can be seen less as the Hegel than as the Antonio Gramsci of American middle-class reform at the turn of the century. Like Gramsci—for whom a robust Communist party would function as a "modern prince," uniting disparate social forces with Machiavellian foresight, ingenuity, and commitment—Croly repudiates the idea that salvation can be achieved "behind the backs," as it were, of its protagonists, through "invisible hands" or "historical forces." What is needed, Croly maintains, is a coordinating purpose and a coordinating agent. The purpose, he avers, is "a more highly socialized democracy [to substitute] . . . for an excessively individualized democracy."[30] The agent is the liberal state, but in a Progressive rather than laissez-faire form, politically empowered to collect and administer federal taxes, including a progressive national income tax, to regulate corporate transactions, banking, and labor relations, and to generate a mildly redistributive social policy designed to mitigate "the social problem."

Croly, in short, endorses a new, hegemonic political project of social and economic reform. Such a project is defended on moral grounds, as a necessary condition of realizing the promise of American life; it is defended on technocratic grounds, as a condition of "associated efficiency" and "efficient government." But above all it is defended on pragmatic grounds, as a way of averting the social and political crisis that is bound to follow if "responsible" and "constructive" action is not taken.

As I elaborate in the next chapter, Progressive reformism was not radical, and indeed was intended in large part to forestall radicalism. But it was in its own way innovative and bold, and it was most assuredly *modernist*. The Progressives were steeped in the most advanced scientific developments of their day, from Darwinian biology to "scientific management." Many of the most influential Progressive writers and activists were university-trained scholars and intellectuals committed to the scientific method and to a comparative understanding of social and political life. As Progressives, as apostles of progress, enlightenment, technical and social *advance*, they were four-square against the cult of American exceptionalism that had long supported America's distinctively Madisonian, decentralist regime, a cult that promoted a narrow and primitivist worship of the Constitution and its fragmentation of power. Croly spoke for most Progressives when he denounced those who subscribe to the "insidious tradition of conformity—the tradition that a patriotic American citizen must not in his political thinking go beyond the formulas consecrated in the sacred American writings. They adhere to the stupefying rule that the good Fathers of the Republic relieved their children from the necessity of vigorous, independent, or consistent thinking in political matters—that it is the duty of their loyal children to repeat the sacred words and then await a miraculous consummation of individual and social prosperity."[31] As I discuss in the next chapter, many Progressives were themselves propelled by religious, largely Christian impulses. But theirs was a distinctively liberal, modernizing religiosity that repudiated a worshipful attitude toward anything—with the important exception of "progress" itself.

The Progressive cast of mind was inconsistent with any kind of obeisance to authority, whether it be theological or constitutional. Fundamentalism of any kind was to be rejected. In this regard the infamous Scopes Trial of 1925 symbolized the open conflict between Progressive commitments and the Christian fundamentalist revival that was in large part directed against these commitments. The "verdict of history," as it were, at least until fairly recently, was clear—Clarence Darrow, in defending the right to teach Darwinian biology in the public schools of Tennessee, spoke on behalf of modernization and "progress" and against obscurantism and reaction. This, at least, was the "Progressive" reading of the matter. For Progressivism, political reform and the creation of a nationalizing, regulatory state was part and parcel of a broader commitment to intellectual progress, technological advance, and the growth of a corporate, consumerist economy capable of generating increasing prosperity for Americans. These forces, on the Progressive view, could not be held back. The only reasonable task, then, was intelligently and responsibly to regulate and thus to promote these developments through the reconstitution of political authority.

THE PROGRESSIVE LEGACY

Progressivism was a complex constellation of forces. It represented a vital and effective reformation of American liberalism, but it was no panacea for America's ills, nor was it a demiurgic force for good. Like all political phenomena, it had its limitations and its weaknesses. Yet it produced important institutional reforms and at an even deeper level advanced a new public philosophy that supported a mildly social democratic, interventionist, and regulatory state. In this way it established precedents and developed intellectual and political resources that could and would be drawn upon in future political struggles as "the American Century" unfolded.

Progressivism was a genuinely idealistic and reformist movement, and it effected important changes in socioeconomic life designed to offset the most glaring and disturbing ill effects of corporate capitalism—urban blight, uncontrolled financial speculation, economic insecurity and inequality. Croly's idea of "a more highly socialized democracy" involved democratization in at least two ways. On the one hand, it involved bringing more aspects of social life under the scope of the democratic authority of the nation-state in the name of political equality. Under the new conditions, Croly saw, meaningful political equality required that those issues of most concern to ordinary American voters—employment conditions, housing conditions, urban planning, public education—must become thoroughly part of the nation's political agenda, and must not be insulated from public, democratic decision making in the name of the sanctity of local tradition or constitutional precedent or the market. In this respect the regulatory state represented a response to the politically articulated demands of ordinary citizens, many of them wage-earners and small producers, who insisted upon the public importance of their problems and demanded that politicians and government officials take them seriously. On the other hand, the regulatory state was conceived as an enablement and support of democratic citizenship itself. For without some legal constraints on corporate conduct, and some provisions for the security of ordinary Americans, the legal and political equality symbolized by the franchise would be of limited value. In both senses, Progressive reform was inherently inclusive and democratic.

Yet, like all forms of democratic innovation, Progressive reform was not without its own forms of exclusion and, in spite of its avowedly democratic aspirations, Progressive equality only went so far. Contemporary celebrants of the Progressive impulse often ignore or downplay these limits, but this is both an historical and a political mistake. For in many ways these limits of Progressivism help us to understand the weakened state of liberalism today.

Perhaps the most important limit of Progressivism was what might be called its culturally assimilationist agenda. As many historians have noted, and as I discuss in the next chapter, Progressivism emerged in large part out of the modernizing, liberal pietist wing of American Protestantism. Progressives promoted urban reforms designed to incorporate and to benefit newly arrived immigrant groups, and advanced an agenda of political reform intended to promote a genuinely national citizenship. Yet most Progressives promoted assimilationism rather than ethnic pluralism. They sought, in other words, to use public policy, especially public education, to dissolve cultural differences in the name of a liberal *American* identity that effaced ethnicity. As Jane Addams maintained: "Americanism was then regarded as a great cultural task and we eagerly sought to invent new instruments and measures by which to undertake it."[32] The "melting pot" model promoted what Michael Lind has called the transition from an "Anglo-Saxon" nation to a "Euro-American" nation.[33]

But this conception of nationality was not without its own forms of exclusion. The constitutional scholar Rogers Smith has highlighted the chauvinism and scientific racism that flourished during the Progressive era, attitudes that helped to fuel the restrictive Immigration Reform Act of 1924.[34] While some Progressives came within the orbit of these beliefs—Theodore Roosevelt springs to mind, and also the sociologist E. A. Ross—many others rejected such racism in the name of a Darwinian universalism of the species. But even here there remained an undercurrent of suspicion toward cultural difference, a suspicion expressed within the idiom of evolutionary anthropology rather than scientific racism, but a suspicion nonetheless. Catholic and Jewish immigrants from Southern and Eastern Europe were often cast as "backward" and "corrupt" by Progressive reformers. Progressives sought to "socialize" foreigners, to incorporate them within conventional middle-class normality, to take the "edge" off of their cultural and political style. Progressive educational reforms sought to undermine the power of ethnic and parochial schools in the name of professional teacher training and certification. The Progressive emphasis on "service," and on the new "helping professions" like social work, similarly promoted a democratic ideology that genuinely sought to include the "unwashed masses," but its concern with "uplift" was also laced with condescension toward ethnic folkways and urban religious practices.

With this consideration in mind, for example, it is possible to read Jane Addams's account of Chicago's Nineteenth Ward, quoted above, in a different, less benevolent light, and the "dirtiness" that it describes can be seen as at once a sociological critique of economic conditions and a moral critique of the "primitive" lifestyles often evidenced by immigrant groups that shades into a kind of cultural chauvinism. C. Wright Mills called attention to this in his characterization of Progressive social thought as a "moralizing sociology of milieux" that centered on "problems of adjustment" to the mores of middle-American, middle-class living. For him the "socialization of immigrants" epitomized this impulse—a distinctively American version of *noblesse oblige*.[35]

Thus, while Progressivism did promote a genuinely national conception of citizenship based on the practice of ethnic assimilation rather than ethnic exclusion, the Progressive conception of "Americanism" was heavily weighted toward a WASP, middle-class worldview. The most important political effect of this bias lay in the area of the Progressive commitment to political reform. In their effort to refashion local and national government and to promote a more activist state, the Progressives also advanced an agenda of political reform designed to attack "special interests" and to promote "good government." "Good government," for Progressive reformers, was government freed from the corrupting influence of privileged elites. One such elite was the corporate elite of "robber barons" who had used their newly gotten wealth to dominate the political process and to forestall beneficial regulatory reforms. Another was the political elite of "bosses" associated with political machines and their power to deliver patronage to supporters. This clientelistic style of politics was especially prevalent in the cities and was an important means of incorporating immigrant groups, whose rural backgrounds made them familiar with clientelism and who often derived advantages from the patronage system instituted by urban political machines. Progressive political reforms attacked this system, and promoted a style of nonpartisanship that was averse to party politics. The city commission and city manager systems of governance were one set of institutional changes designed to achieve this result. The plebiscitary practice of initiatives and referenda was another. But perhaps the most important such reforms were a series of electoral devices designed to purify political conflict and to free it of its partisanship and zealousness—the Australian ballot (replacing the long-standing use of partisan ballots); secret voting; antifusion laws designed to limit the power of third parties; and new literacy requirements for voting. These reforms were presented in the name of "cleaning up" the political process and making it more reflective of an unadulterated public opinion. And, in many ways, these reforms accomplished just this, and did represent serious efforts to promote democratic citizenship and in particular to limit the power of money in politics.[36] But their effect was also to substantially weaken urban political machines and to severely limit the electoral participation of the lower classes.[37]

This was especially true for African Americans, who were disenfranchised by the passage of literacy laws and grandfather clauses in every Southern state between the years 1890 and 1920. The era of Progressivism was also the era of the final, formal repudiation of Reconstruction and the introduction of Jim Crow in the American South, marked by the famous 1896 Supreme Court decision in *Plessy v. Ferguson*. This reinstitution of virtual slavery for Southern African Americans is surely the darkest side of the Progressive era. This is of course a complex story, and it would be simply wrong to imply that all Progressives were racist or that institutional racism was a conscious goal of Progressive reform. But it would be equally misleading to ignore the fact that on balance Progressivism made its peace with the forces of racial reaction and even more misleading to ignore the important historical consequences of this fateful choice. For, as I argue below, American liberalism in the twentieth century has been indelibly tarnished by its complacency in the face of racial injustice, and indeed for its complicity in such injustice.

Closely linked to the demobilizing effects of political reform was a technocratic impulse central to Progressive reformism, something emphasized in the so-called corporate liberal interpretation of Progressivism that rose to prominence in the United States during the sixties. "Associated efficiency" was a core value continually reiterated in the works of Croly, Lippmann, Weyl, and other Progressive writers and publicists. In economics, the large-scale industrial corporation, with its "scientific management" of labor and its enlightened industrial statesmanship, was viewed by Progressives as an indispensable vehicle of progress when properly constrained by a regulatory state. And such an administrative state, based on a reformed, bureaucratized civil service, was similarly viewed as the principal means of regulating social and economic life. In their quest to rationalize society and to tame the new, destabilizing forces associated with industrialization, immigration, and urbanization, Progressives placed extraordinary faith in the intellectual and political capacities of large-scale, bureaucratic institutions in general and state institutions in particular.[38]

This faith was no more in evidence than in the years immediately following U.S. entry into World War I, when Progressives embraced Wilson's war aims and *The New Republic* waged an all-out campaign on behalf of the war's "progressive" tendencies. This sorry episode in the history of American liberalism has been recounted in numerous histories. The basic outlines of the story are simple. Progressives, including Croly, Lippmann, Weyl, and especially Dewey, saw the war as an opportunity to promote a sense of "national purpose" that could be harnessed in peacetime to promote socioeconomic reform and a corporatist model of "industrial democracy"; and they viewed the bureaucratic agencies established to prosecute the war as exemplars of a reformed, regulatory state.

As Robert Westbrook has shown in his *John Dewey and American Democracy*, Dewey in particular placed his commitment to pragmatist experimentalism in the service of the war effort, arguing that the war had set in motion progressive tendencies that true pragmatists should seek to harness rather than to reject in the manner of "absolutist" pacifists and antimilitarists. Like Lippmann in *Drift and Mastery*, Dewey believed the job of the true progressive was not to resist emerging historical forces but to tame and to master them, to direct them toward "progressive" ends.[39] In his brilliant book *The Crossroads of Liberalism*, Charles Forcey documents this Machiavellian moment within Progressive liberalism, and shows how this credulousness about power and this belief on the part of Progressive intellectuals that they were riding a wave of historical progress was dashed by the actual course of the war, by its mobilization of jingoism, by the massive repression and Red Scare that it called into being, and especially by its failure to "make the world safe for democracy" in the way that it had promised.[40] As Forcey shows, the outcome of the war generated a serious crisis of confidence for progressives. Walter Weyl spoke for many when he wrote, in his diary, that the war "has rudely shattered my optimism concerning the progress of humanity."[41] He died a few months later, disillusioned with liberalism and fascinated by the Bolshevik triumph in Russia. Some Progressives, like Lippmann, turned toward a more jaded form of *realpolitick*, abandoning their earlier idealism entirely. Others, like Croly, turned away from politics and toward culture, aesthetics, or religion. Still others, like Dewey, emerged from the war with their liberal commitments tested and strengthened. As Westbrook demonstrates, Dewey came to see the errors of his earlier support of the war and developed a searching critique of his earlier credulousness. Recognizing the dangers of militarism and bureaucratic government, in 1920 he joined—with Jane Addams, Roger Baldwin, Clarence Darrow, Felix Frankfurter, Norman Thomas, and others—to help establish the American Civil Liberties Union. And in his postwar political writings he developed a conception of public philosophy that was robustly reformist and democratic.

As the example of Dewey shows, Progressive liberalism was not extinguished by the war. But it did not survive unscathed. Indeed, one can go further. While Progressive impulses and ideas persisted, Progressivism as a movement of socioeconomic and political reform did not survive the war. In part this was due to changing intellectual styles. As C. Wright Mills has argued, after the war the "liberal practicality" of Progressivism became increasingly bureaucratic, instrumentalist, and illiberal. In his polemical essay "Twilight of the Idols," Randolph Bourne described this new intellectual ethos:

> The war has revealed a younger intelligentsia, trained up in the pragmatic dispensation, immensely ready for the executive ordering of events, pitifully unprepared for the intellectual interpretation or the idealistic focussing of ends . . . [Dewey's] disciples have learned all too literally the instrumental attitude toward life and, being immensely intelligent and energetic, they are making themselves efficient instruments of the war technique, accepting with little question the ends as announced from above. That those ends are largely negative does not concern them, because they have never learned not to subordinate idea to technique. Their education has not given them a coherent system of large ideas, or a feeling for democratic goals. They have, in short, no clear philosophy of life except that of intelligent service, the admirable adaptation of means to ends. . . . They have absorbed the secret of scientific administration as applied to political administration.[42]

For Bourne, this new intellectual dispensation had betrayed the earlier idealism of Progressivism, abandoning a vision of social reform and making its peace with corporate capitalism and the bureaucratic state. Bourne's critique highlights a profound irony of Progressivism—while Progressives understood themselves to be enlightened critics of a politics of elites and "special interests," in many ways they constituted *themselves* as a political elite, empowered by their connections to new scientific, bureaucratic, and statist institutions, and by their rhetorical disparagement of more populistic approaches to the state, to modernity, and to questions of war and peace. Bourne's critique would be recuperated in the 1960s by New Left critics of liberalism *and* by New Right critics equally opposed to liberalism's technocratic bent. For both groups, the "original sin" of modern day liberalism lay in its surreptitious elitism.

Just as important as the *traison de clercs* in explaining the post-World War I decline of Progressivism was the fact that the wartime mobilization and repression had extinguished those radical impulses that had fueled progressive reform in the first place, something I discuss in the next chapter. The postwar period—the "Roaring Twenties" of popular parlance—was thus a period of corporate dominance, economic prosperity and growing consumerism, and political conservatism.

Yet Progressivism survived, in the form of the institutional innovations it had inspired and in the memories of many of its protagonists. While it is beyond the scope of my argument to offer a detailed history of Progressivism's subsequent career, it is absolutely essential to appreciate its continuing legacy for, as I asserted earlier, Progressivism laid the foundation for the subsequent evolution of twentieth-century American liberalism. While the New Deal, for instance, went beyond the Progressive example in important ways—its unambiguous embrace of lower-class ethnic voters, its support for the full-fledged mobilization of the working class and its codification of labor rights, the extensive welfare state that it established—the essential Progressivism of New Deal liberalism is beyond question, something that is acknowledged by virtually every important history of the period from Arthur Schlesinger Jr.'s *The Age of Roosevelt* to Alan Brinkley's *The End of Reform*.[43] Franklin Delano Roosevelt's "Brain Trust" was steeped in Progressive ideas and many of them had had prior political and administrative experience during the Progressive era. Perhaps no one epitomized this more than Adolph Berle, a principal Roosevelt advisor. Berle, along with Gardiner Means, coauthored *The Modern Corporation and Private Property* (1932), a veritable bible of New Deal reformism.[44] He also drafted FDR's famous "Commonwealth Club Address" of 1932, in which Roosevelt laid out his ambitious program of socioeconomic reform based on the idea of economic rights and "social security." Indeed, as the historian Robert Eden has shown, in drafting this speech Berle quite self-consciously reappropriated the themes of John Dewey's *Individualism Old and New* (1930), a book that deliberately sought to apply Progressive ideas to the conditions of the Depression-era United States.[45]

To insist on the Progressivism of New Deal reforms is not to belie the rhetorical and ideological complexity of the New Deal period nor to deny the important policy shifts that characterized its various phases. There is a well-established historical consensus that the "New Deal liberalism" that emerged after the end of World War II was quite different—more conservative, more consumerist—than the more ambitious, fractious, frankly radical liberalism of the earlier New Deal period. But the existence of such discontinuities does not gainsay the importance of historical continuities, especially at the level of rhetoric and public discourse.[46] In this regard it seems beyond question that the liberalism that survived WWII furthered the essentially Crolyean conception of an activist, regulatory state seeking to solve "the social problem" in its various incarnations.

A similar argument could be made about the Great Society reforms of the Kennedy-Johnson administration. Here too the federal government attempted an extensive series of socioeconomic reforms—Medicare and Medicaid, Head Start, a "war on poverty" spearheaded by the Office of Economic Opportunity, etc.—designed to ameliorate problems of poverty and inequality and in so doing to address what Croly called "the social problem." Here too, of course, matters are complex, something to which I return below, in considering the legacies of the sixties. For there can be no denying the radical nature of sixties cultural politics, which surpassed—and transgressed—the boundaries of Progressive liberalism, and brought forth demands, and remedies, that severely challenged, and ultimately weakened, this liberalism. But even here it is undeniable that the rhetoric of the Johnson administration, and the conception of activist government on which it drew, was in large part drawn from the repertoire of Progressive liberalism, and further testifies to the enduring legacy of Progressivism.

To insist on this legacy, once again, is not to maintain an implausible thesis about the demiurgic power of Progressive liberalism. Progressivism is not and has not been an essential or unchanging phenomenon, and it does not propel itself through history of its own accord. Rather, it is a complex tradition of rhetoric, ideas, and policies that has been drawn upon, and reshaped, by successive generations of activists, politicians, and policy makers. That this tradition has been both inspirational and extraordinarily productive seems beyond doubt. Contemporary neoprogressives are understandably drawn to it. Indeed, the more adamant conservatives become in decrying government, social policy, and reformist idealism, and insisting that the voluntarism of the church, neighborhood, and marketplace is the answer to all our problems, the more appealing the Progressive tradition becomes, for it stands for inquiry rather than conventional dogma, and intelligent action rather than complacency and drift.

It is impossible for me to read the early Croly or Lippmann, or Dewey's *Liberalism and Social Action* (1935), or Lyndon Johnson's famous Howard University "War on Poverty" address, and not experience a shiver of excitement, for these texts express an exuberant idealism that borders on willfulness, but also a generosity of spirit, and a commitment to serious political work, that is so far removed from the current discourse of American politics. Every year I show parts of the PBS documentary "America's War on Poverty" to my undergraduates. They watch, and listen to, LBJ, and RFK, and Sargeant Shriver, as these men talk with conviction about how the right social policies can improve cities, or the lives of the elderly, or race relations. These individuals are throwbacks to another era, in which policy intellectuals and political elites thought differently, entertained more ambitious ideas about what was politically feasible, and were able to give public voice to such ideas.[47] To observe this is not to lionize the Great Society era, nor the Progressive tradition that inspired it. As I have tried to indicate below, these Progressive reformers were not unblemished, and indeed the history of American Progressive liberalism in the twentieth century is a history of compromises with corporate capitalism, racial injustice, and bureaucratic statism.

Nonetheless it is also a history of substantial and beneficial social change, and in this regard it truly *is* an exemplary history. The revival of Progressivism today would not be an unmixed blessing. But a blessing it would be. For it would reinstate the idea that public problems require public solutions, and that organized, social intelligence is a necessary force for human and civic betterment. Neoprogressives are right about this. Where they are wrong is in vastly overestimating the likelihood of such a revival. For while neoprogressives correctly note similarities between the challenges confronting us today and those that confronted earlier Progressives, they fail to appreciate the historical and sociological distance that separates us from Progressivism. The appeal to Progressivism is attractive, but it is also deeply anachronistic. It is to this issue that I now turn.

NOTES

1. E. J. Dionne Jr., *They Only Look Dead: Why Progressives Will Dominate the Next Century* (New York: Simon and Schuster, 1996), p. 12.

2. See Robert H. Wiebe, *The Search for Order, 1877–1920* (New York: Hill and Wang, 1967).

3. Carl Degler, *Out of Our Past* (New York: Harper, 1970), pp. 238–40.

4. On the power of the steel industry, see William Serrin's *Homestead: The Glory and Tragedy of an American Steel Town* (New York: Times Books, 1992).

5. See Wiebe, *The Search for Order*, pp. 115–28.

6. See Degler, *Out of Our Past*, pp. 243–50.

7. Henry George, "Progress and Poverty," in Leon Fink, ed., *Major Problems of the Gilded Age and the Progressive Era* (Lexington, MA: D. C. Heath, 1993), pp. 5–6.

8. Quoted in Bernard Bailyn et al., *The Great Republic: A History of the American People*, vol. 2 (Lexington, MA: D. C. Heath, 1985), p. 598.

9. Karl Marx and Friedrich Engels, "Manifesto of the Communist Party," in *Collected Works, vol. 6: 1845–1848* (New York: International Publishers, 1976), p. 489.

10. Degler, *Out of Our Past*, p. 362.

11. The summary below draws heavily from Harold Underwood Faulkner, *The Quest for Social Justice, 1898–1914* (New York: Macmillan, 1931). See also John D. Buenker, *Urban Liberalism and Progressive Reform* (New York: Scribners, 1973).

12. Quoted in Morton Keller, *Regulating a New Society: Public Policy and Social Change in America, 1900–1933* (Cambridge, MA: Harvard University Press, 1994), p. 50.

13. See Lawrence Cremin, *The Transformation of the American School: Progressivism in American Education, 1876–1957* (New York: Random House, 1961).

14. See Steven Skowronek, *Building a New American State: The Expansion of National Administrative Capacities, 1877–1920* (Cambridge: Cambridge University Press, 1982); Keller, *Regulating a New Society,* op. cit.; Martin J. Sklar, *The Corporate Reconstruction of American Capitalism, 1890–1916: The Market, The Law, and Politics* (Cambridge: Cambridge University Press, 1988); and Eldon J. Eisenach, *The Lost Promise of Progressivism* (Lawrence, KS: University Press of Kansas, 1994).

15. Root quoted in Sklar, *The Corporate Reconstruction,* pp. 336–37; Stimson quoted in Arthur J. Schlesinger Jr., *The Age of Roosevelt: The Crisis of the Old Order, 1919–1933* (Boston: Houghton Mifflin, 1957), p. 19.

16. Kevin Mattson, *Creating a Democratic Public: The Struggle for Urban Participatory Democracy During the Progressive Era* (University Park, PA: Pennsylvania State University Press, 1998).

17. This is major theme of Eisenach's *Lost Promise of Progressivism* (Lawrence, KS: University Press of Kansas, 1994). Eisenach concludes from this that the actual policy regime that developed was not authentically Progressive.

18. Walter Lippmann, *Drift and Mastery* (New York: M. Kennerley, 1914), p. 18.

19. Morton White, *Social Thought in America: The Revolt Against Formalism* (New York: Viking Press, 1949), p. 13.

20. John Dewey, "The Need for a Recovery in Philosophy," in Debra Morriss and Ian Shapiro, eds., *John Dewey: The Political Writings* (Indianapolis: Hackett, 1993), p. 9.

21. Quoted in John Patrick Diggins, *The Promise of Pragmatism* (Chicago: University of Chicago Press, 1994), pp. 9–10.

22. Quoted in White, *Social Thought in America,* p. 55.

23. Quoted in John William Ward, "Introduction" to Herbert Croly, *The Promise of American Life* (Indianapolis: Bobbs-Merrill, 1965), p. viii.

24. Quoted in Degler, *Out of Our Past,* p. 363.

25. Quoted in Thomas Hill Green, "Negative and Positive Freedom," in Carl Cohen, ed., *Communism, Fascism and Democracy* (New York: Random House, 1972), pp. 485–87.

26. See James T. Kloppenberg, *Uncertain Victory: Social Democracy and Progressivism in European and American Thought, 1870–1920* (Oxford: Oxford University Press, 1986).

27. On Croly's influence, see Eric F. Goldman's classic *Rendezvous with Destiny* (New York: Knopf, 1958); Charles Forcey, *The Crossroads of Liberalism: Croly, Weyl, Lippmann and the Progressive Era, 1900–1925* (Oxford: Oxford University Press, 1961); and Edward A. Stettner, *Shaping Modern Liberalism: Herbert Croly and Progressive Thought* (Lawrence, KS: Kansas University Press, 1993).

28. Croly, *The Promise,* p. 17.

29. Croly, *The Promise,* p. 139.

30. Croly, *The Promise,* p. 25.

31. Croly, *The Promise,* p. 150.

32. Quoted in Rivkah Shpak-Lisak, *Pluralism and Progressives: Hull House and the New Immigrants* (Chicago: University of Chicago Press, 1989).

33. Michael Lind, *The Next American Nation* (New York: Free Press, 1995), pp. 74–85.

34. Rogers Smith, *Civic Ideals: Conflicting Views of Citizenship in U.S. History* (New Haven, CT: Yale University Press, 1997).

35. C. Wright Mills, *The Sociological Imagination* (Oxford: Oxford University Press, 1959), pp. 88–92. See also Christopher Lasch, "The Politics of Social Control," in his *The New Radicalism in America: 1889–1963* (New York: Knopf, 1965). For a more nuanced and appreciative account of the assimilationist politics of Jane Addams, emphasizing the generosity of her commitments, see Jean Elshtain, *Jane Addams and the Dream of American Democracy* (New York: Basic Books, 2001).

36. See Kevin Mattson, *Creating a Democratic Public: The Struggle for Participatory Democracy During the Progressive Era* (University Park, PA: Pennsylvania State Press, 1998); and Peter Levine, *The New Progressive Era: Toward a Fair and Deliberative Democracy* (Totowa, NJ: Rowman & Littlefield, 2000).

37. See American Social History Project, *Who Built America?* (New York: Pantheon, 1992), pp. 200–204; Michael E. McGerr, *The Decline of Popular Politics: The American North, 1865–1928* (Oxford: Oxford University Press, 1985), and Kenneth Finegold, *Experts and Politicians: Reform Challenges to Machine Politics in New York, Cleveland, and Chicago* (Princeton, NJ: Princeton University Press, 1969). Kevin Mattson offers a more favorable gloss on some of these Progressive reformist impulses in his *Creating a Democratic Public*.

38. See Robert H. Wiebe, *The Search for Order, 1877–1920* (New York: Hill and Wang, 1967).

39. Robert B. Westbrook, *John Dewey and American Democracy* (Ithaca, NY: Cornell University Press, 1991), pp. 195–230.

40. Charles Forcey, *The Crossroads of Liberalism: Croly, Weyl, Lippmann and the Progressive Era, 1900–1925* (Oxford: Oxford University Press, 1961), pp. 221–316. See also Stuart Ewen's account of George Creel's role as head of Wilson's Committee on Public Information, set up to propagandize on behalf of the American war effort, in Ewen, *PR: A Social History of Spin* (New York: Basic Books, 1996), pp. 105–27.

41. Forcey, *The Crossroads of Liberalism*, p. 295.

42. Randolph Bourne, "Twilight of Idols," in *War and the Intellectuals: Collected Essays, 1915–1919* (New York: Harper Torchbooks, 1964), pp. 59–60.

43. See Arthur M. Schlesinger Jr., *The Age of Roosevelt: The Crisis of the Old Order, 1919–1933* (Boston: Houghton Mifflin, 1957), and Alan Brinkley, *The End of Reform: New Deal Liberalism in Recession and War* (New York: Vintage, 1995).

44. Adolf A. Berle and Gardner C. Means, *Modern Corporation and Private Property* (New York: Corporation Trust Company, 1932).

45. See Robert Eden, "'On The Origins of Liberalism': John Dewey, Adolph A. Berle, and FDR's Commonwealth Club Address of 1932," *Studies in American Political Development*, vol. 7, no. 1 (spring 1993), pp. 74–150.

46. On these issues, see Michael K. Brown, "The Ambiguity of Reform in the New Deal," Kenneth Finegold, "Ideology and Institutions in the End of Reform," and especially David Plotke, "The Endurance of New Deal Liberalism," all contributions to an interesting forum on Brinkley's book published in *Studies in American Political Development*, vol. 10 (fall 1996), pp. 405–20; see also Ira Katznelson and Bruce Pietrykowski, "Rebuilding the American State: Evidence from the 1940's," *Studies in American Political Development*, vol. 5 (fall 1991).

47. Peter Edelman's recent *Searching for America's Heart: RFK and the Renewal of Hope* (Boston: Houghton Mifflin, 2001) emphasizes the power of this idealism, and how far we have fallen away from it.

3

+

The World We Have Lost

Progressivism, then, has been an enormously productive idiom of political praxis that has shaped American public philosophy and public policy in the twentieth century. As I have argued, Progressivism at its inception was distinguished by its resolute modernism and by its commitment to *public action* rather than "drift" or faith in invisible hands, historical inevitabilities, or providential interventions. In this regard it possessed a strong dose of voluntarism. Nonetheless Progressives forswore what they considered "utopian" or "radical" solutions, insisting, in the words of Lippmann, that Progressive reforms should be grounded in, and supportive of, "the promise of actual things." Progressive ideas, and the reforms that they inspired and supported, thus constituted an impressive and vital "superstructure" based on the actual processes of modernization that were transforming American society at the turn of the century.

These processes fueled Progressive reform and buoyed the historical optimism of the early Progressives, and their continued unfolding as the century progressed similarly fueled subsequent episodes of liberal reformism. It is this synergy between social modernization and Progressive reform that is ignored by almost all current advocates of a Progressive revival. These advocates fail to come to terms with the fact that while our era parallels the Progressive era in the magnitude of the problems and the need for public responses that it presents, the *character* of these problems is quite dissimilar. The social world at the dawn of the twenty-first century does not support liberal reformism in the way that the world at the dawn of the twentieth century did. If Progressivism was

77

a public philosophy for a modernizing nation, our current predicament, I argue, calls for a new political orientation appropriate to a period that many have labeled *postmodern*.

Let me be clear here. I am not putting forth a thesis of radical discontinuity between past and present. Nor am I aligning myself with a philosophy of "postmodernism," a nebulous term often deployed as an epithet in academic culture wars. But I do mean to call attention to certain important structural and cultural changes that American society has undergone in the past quarter century, and broadly to consider the implications of these changes for progressive and neoprogressive politics. I have in mind such things as the turn to postindustrial and "post-Fordist" forms of production and accumulation; the emergence of new fault lines of social conflict that displace class; the development and deployment of new modes of communication and obfuscation; and what Jurgen Habermas has called "the exhaustion of utopian possibilities" associated with the crisis of the welfare state. If at the dawn of the twentieth century the "promise of actual things" supported Progressive aspirations, current social tendencies do not auger as well for such aspirations, and indeed promise less to fuel than to frustrate them. Or so I argue.

One more caveat is in order. The argument of this chapter is that Progressivism flourished at the turn of the last century because of a supportive social environment. This argument is vaguely functionalist in its insistence on the structural enablements and limits of political action. In making this argument I do not in any way wish to imply that social conditions or structural imperatives "cause" political developments in any simple-minded sense. Progressivism represented a creative intellectual and political effort to respond to social conditions, and it succeeded in large part because of its ingenuity. In politics ideas, strategies, and convictions matter tremendously. Modernizing social conditions did not necessitate Progressive reform early in the century, and the absence of such conditions today does not necessarily doom the current effort to revive Progressivism. But these conditions do impose important constraints, and call into question some of the underlying assumptions of a contemporary Progressive revival. Latter day progressives may summon an optimism of the will, and indeed such a willful optimism may inspire some noble efforts. But if I am correct the world in which we live is likely to frustrate such an optimism.

The principal modernizing forces in Progressive era America were the socioeconomic changes alluded to in the previous chapter—industrialization, and the processes of urbanization and mass immigration that accompanied it. These changes dramatically transformed American life, presenting new opportunities for organizing social interaction and also generating daunting challenges of coordination and social justice that fueled Progressive reform.

Progressive political and social reform represented merely the tip of an iceberg of underlying social changes. Among these changes a few loomed largest in terms of their broad political importance. Simply to name them is to mark the difference between that world and our own.

THE ASCENDANCY OF LIBERAL PROTESTANTISM

As scholars have understood at least as far back as the "modernization" literature of the 1960s, one of the most important effects of industrialization and urbanization is to promote the "secularization" of social life. By secularization I mean here not the withering away of religious belief and practice but the desacralization of society and the corresponding liberalization of religious attitudes, practices, and agendas.

American society at the end of the nineteenth century was a society suffused with a Protestant Christianity, tracing its lineage back to early Puritanism, that was assailed by the forces of social, economic, and intellectual modernity. Traditional beliefs about creation, the divinely inspired authority of Scripture, the historical Jesus, and the finality of Christianity were thrown into question by developments in Darwinian biology that affected every sphere of intellectual life, from history, anthropology, and psychology to metaphysics and theology. The development of new forms of interdependence and vulnerability profoundly challenged the theological individualism of traditional Protestant and especially Calvinist doctrine regarding individual salvation through personal faith. Beyond these threats to the intellectual integrity of religious praxis, urbanization, and its disruption of small-town mores, combined with the influx of millions of predominantly Catholic and Jewish immigrants, called into question the very institutional relevance of the Protestant churches.

In response to these challenges American Protestantism underwent a veritable conversion experience. Under the leadership of theologians such as Lyman Abbott and Horace Bushnell, Protestant churches developed a more liberal theology, sometimes called "Progressive Orthodoxy," that sought to reconcile Christian faith with the scientific methods, and conclusions, of evolutionary biology and psychology, and to emphasize God's *immanence* in the natural and human world. On this view the importance of man's inherent sinfulness recedes, and the perfectibility of man and of society is raised to a principle of ethical and religious centrality. Progressive orthodoxy thus licensed an emphasis on worldly improvement and on human brotherhood and community, and it viewed the social disruptions and inequalities engendered by modernization as spurs to intelligent social action rather than as divinely furnished tests of individual or communal spiritual fidelity.

This impulse was taken even further by the Social Gospel movement that swept through American society in the latter decades of the nineteenth century. Ministers such as Josiah Strong, Washington Gladden, George D. Herron, and Walter Rauschenbusch preached a *social* rather than an individualist gospel, insisting that the good and righteous Christian must actively seek to realize Christian principles of love, mercy, and brotherhood by challenging the inequalities associated with industrial capitalism. As Steven C. Rockefeller has written:

> [the Social Gospel movement] endeavored to transform the church into an instrument of social betterment in the belief that any program to save individuals must involve social reform. The Social Gospel theologians attacked the extreme individualism of much evangelical religion, arguing that individuals do not exist as isolated entities but as members of a social order that profoundly shapes their habits and character. They generally rejected the doctrine of original sin and maintained faith in the perfectability of human nature, believing that the power of moral evil can be subdued in and through the reform of social conditions. They shared in a widespread social belief in progress. For them realization of the kingdom of God on earth was a real hope and inspiration. In all of this the liberals were expressing the major shift in cultural mood that marked the emergence of modern urban industrial society . . . a shift of controlling interest from other-wordly salvation of the soul to a this-worldly realization of well-being and fulfillment.[1]

The Social Gospel emphasis on this-worldly fulfillment through progressive social action may have been lacking in theological rigor or strenuousness (Jean Elshtain recently has leveled this criticism against liberal Protestantism), but there can be no doubt about either its idealism or its profound social importance.[2] Books such as George D. Herron's *The New Redemption: A Call to the Church to Reconstruct Society According to the Gospel of Christ* (1893) and Washington Gladden's *Applied Christianity: Moral Aspects of the Social Question* (1896) helped to shape the preaching and the ministries of hundreds of mainline Protestant churches during the Progressive era; and more popularly oriented Social Gospel texts, like William T. Stead's *If Christ Came to Chicago: A Plea for the Union of All Who Love in the Service of All Who Suffer* (1894) and Charles M. Sheldon's *In His Steps: Or, What Would Jesus Do?* (1896), were genuine best-sellers, the latter experiencing a print run of more than 20 *million* copies.[3]

These texts, and the ideas they promulgated, were influential beyond the sphere of religious thinking and action narrowly conceived. Just as the society as a whole was suffused with Protestant Christianity and challenged spiritually and liturgically by the onset of modernization, so too the society as a whole was influenced by the development and spread of liberal Protestantism. Eldon Eisenach nicely described the growing hegemony of liberal Protestantism. As he writes:

> Spurred on by the New Theology and the social gospel, evangelical Protestantism rapidly expanded its power and reach through its thriving system of universities, colleges, divinity schools, and its newly formed city and state federations, culminating in 1908 in the founding of the Federal Council of Churches of Christ in America. New parachurch organizations were also created or expended at this time: Christian youth and student movements, settlement houses, mission training societies, and a host of social action organizations.[4]

As has been commonly acknowledged, the writings of Progressive social scientists such as Richard T. Ely, Albion Small, George Herbert Mead, and E. A. Ross were infused with liberal Protestant themes, as witnessed by very the title of Ross's seminal book *Sin and Society*.[5] The same is true of the early writings of John Dewey, something most evident in his "Christianity and Democracy," originally presented in 1892 as a lay sermon to the Students' Christian Association of the University of Michigan (the Association was a regular venue for Dewey, who taught Sunday school there for many years). "It is in democracy, the community of ideas and interest through community of action," Dewey argued, "that the incarnation of God in man . . . becomes a living, present thing."[6]

This belief that social democratization and progressive reform were continuous with and indeed mandated by Christian social teaching was widespread. Perhaps its most significant embodiment was the settlement house movement pioneered by Jane Addams, Florence Kelley, and other women reformers (including the Jewish Lillian Wald). Settlements like Hull House in Chicago and the Henry Street Settlement in New York served as social, cultural, and educational centers for working people, mostly immigrant; they also served as nerve centers of progressive reform. Settlement houses were both incubators and agitators for the urban reforms—public health, education, child care—described in the previous chapter. Robert Crumden was quite deliberate in his description of the academic, journalistic, and political activists centered around the settlement house movement as *Ministers of Reform*; and his classic account intends, I think, to underscore both the "political" sense in which these activists functioned as "ministers" of a kind of unofficial "shadow government" composed of nongovernmental institutions; and the religious sense in which they were inspired by ministers and indeed themselves performed a ministerial role, as public philosophers, preachers, and moralists, pricking the conscience of the nation, serving, in the words of Eldon Eisenach, as a "lay clerisy."[7]

The liberalization of Protestant spirituality and social teaching was an absolutely crucial ingredient of the modernizing impulses behind Progressive reform. There could have been no Progressivism had there not been such a liberalization of religion in America, and had religious and religiously based institutions not served as powerful vehicles of Progressive ideas. Yet if at the dawn of the twentieth century liberal religiosity was ascendant, today it seems politically in abeyance if not in decline, supplanted by the rise of fundamentalist forms of religiosity—forms that take their bearings explicitly from earlier fundamentalisms that arose in reaction to Progressivism—the most significant of which is surely the so-called New Christian Right.[8]

It would be an error to exaggerate the influence of the New Christian Right. But it would be equally erroneous to ignore its impact. It remains probably the most well-organized and politically mobilized constituency of the Republican party, and it has exercised influence well beyond its numbers in the Republican primary process—particularly in the South, where state and local parties are dominated by Christian conservatives—and through this influence, it has profoundly shaped national political discourse. According to a 1994 study by *Campaigns and Elections*, the Christian Right exercises a dominant influence over eighteen (out of fifty) state Republican party organizations, where dominant is defined as possessing a working majority of party delegates; and exercises a substantial, i.e., plurality, influence over another thirteen party organizations. In a full 60 percent of the Republican organizations, then, the Christian Right has attained substantial influence.[9]

Beyond this strategic influence within the Republican primary is its extensive organizational infrastructure. The Christian Coalition's membership and influence may have been exaggerated by its publicists of the mid-1990s, but it is nonetheless true that is has organized hundreds of local chapters, distributes its monthly newsletter "The Christian American" to hundreds of thousands of Christian households every month, and distributes millions of voter guides every November. The Christian Coalition *is* a grassroots movement that currently has no analogue on the left. Most of this grassroots development took place under the directorship of Ralph Reed, who once described the Coalition as "the MacDonald's of American politics" because of its ability to spawn local "franchises." Reed's philosophy was summed up in his observation that "the future of America is not [shaped] by who sits in the Oval Office but by who sits in the principal's office."[10]

The Coalition is not alone in this grassroots approach to movement-building. Beverly LaHaye's Concerned Women of America—which claims to be "the largest public policy women's organization" in the United States—boasts a membership of over 500,000 women. The Reverend James Dobson's Focus on the Family employs over a thousand people, who produce 10 magazines that reach over 2.3 million households every month; and Dobson's radio show is broadcast on over 4,000 stations. These organizations, and many others like them, reach out to a broad segment of the American public, through churches, pamphlets, and magazines, and via the air waves and cable television.[11]

The contrast with the spirit—and spirituality—of Progressive era America could not be sharper. If at the turn of the century politically radical books like William Stead's *If Christ Came to Chicago* and George D. Herron's *The New Redemption* were best sellers, today's Christian best sellers, taking a leaf from Hal Lindsay's apocalyptic *The Late, Great Planet Earth*, are books such as the Reverend Pat Robertson's *New World Order* (1991), a *New York Times* Best Seller that has sold well over 500,000 copies, and the blockbuster series about the end of days by Tim LaHaye and Jerry Jenkins, each of which has sold over 500,000 copies, and one of which—*Left Behind*—has sold well over 1 million copies and has been turned into a widely distributed motion picture.[12] These books are to Social Gospel texts what Jacqueline Susann novels are to those of John Dos Passos, Theodore Dreiser, and William Allen White. They represent what is truly a mass market in Christian pulp fiction. Whereas liberal Protestant texts promoted a perfectionist program of social reform and an ethos of communitarian citizenship, these premillennial fantasies present a harsh, Manichean universe that is being propelled toward apocalyptic destruction by the forces of Darwinism, feminism, and liberalism writ large. And these texts indeed *embrace* such destruction as a moment on the path toward salvation.

Such texts contribute to a spirit of antihumanism that is pervasive in our culture, a theme to which I return below. It is not my intention to suggest that the New Christian Right and its extensive popular culture has "Christianized" America or has achieved intellectual or even religious dominance in American society, for this would surely be incorrect. But it is I think undeniable that these forces have achieved considerable "momentum," and that they have helped to nourish a culture in which science, liberalism, and progressive social policy are under a deep cloud of suspicion. Beyond this, they have contributed immensely to the profound cultural polarization of American political discourse, a development that such Progressives as E. J. Dionne and Todd Gitlin concede has helped seriously to weaken liberalism. The hegemony of the Christian Right within the conservative movement has played a crucial role in shaping a political agenda in which abortion, homosexuality, Washington "elitism," and welfare dependency are linked together as symptoms of liberal power and American decline, and in which these cultural and symbolic issues have displaced the distributional concerns of Progressive liberalism at the heart of the national political agenda. The network of religious and religiously based institutions that comprise the Christian Right is thus a principal force behind the delegitimation of American liberalism. And the legacy of over twenty years of activism, much less the continued influence of these conservative Christian forces, constitutes a powerful obstacle to the revival of such a liberalism.

LIBERAL PRACTICALITY AND THE GROWTH OF PROGRESSIVE SOCIAL SCIENCE

Along with the rise of liberal Protestantism, the late nineteenth century saw the birth of the modern research university, heralded by the founding of Cornell University in 1867, the Johns Hopkins University in 1876, and the University of Chicago in 1891. Along with this development came the rise of Ph.D. programs, the dramatic increase in the number of graduate students, and the professionalization of newly established social science disciplines, marked by the founding of the American Economic Association (AEA, 1885), the American Academy of Political and Social Science (1890), the American Philosophical Association (1901), the American Sociological Association (1905), and the American Political Science Association (1906).

It is perhaps hard to imagine given their current complexion, but these disciplines were at their inception deeply reformist, rejecting the formalism of classical learning for an engaged, experimental, problem-solving, and meliorist form of social inquiry. Richard T. Ely, for example, the founder of the American Economic Association, was a Christian-socialist activist who proclaimed that "whenever we truly advance the interests of wage-earners we necessarily advance the interests of all society"; and the founding platform of the AEA announced that "we regard the state as an educational and ethical agency whose positive aid is an indispensable condition of human progress."[13] A similar commitment to Progressive reform animated the disciplines of sociology and political science, the former focusing on problems of "social control" and "socialization" confronting a rapidly changing society infused with new immigrant groups, the latter centered on the limits of oligarchical partisan competition, and on the development of state administrative capacities commensurate with the fulfillment of genuinely "public" functions.

The newly formed social science disciplines carved out distinctive intellectual and professional agendas, but were joined by an ethos of communitarian citizenship and by the commitment to the idea that scientific knowledge could and should serve as an agent of social betterment. Disciplinary founders by and large subscribed to what Harry Boyte has called the doctrine of "civic professionalism"; the professional expertise and autonomy that they sought to develop was understood to have broader public consequences and responsibilities, and professionalism thus involved a genuine civic vocation and was not viewed simply a means of regulating and maintaining occupational privilege or career advancement.[14]

Indeed, the emerging social science disciplines developed in close connection with middle-class reform movements. Books such as Kathryn Kish Sklar's *Florence Kelley and the Nation's Work* and Ellen Fitzpatrick's *Endless Crusade: Women Social Scientists and Progressive Reform*, for example, explore the synergy between a new generation of female scholar-academics like Florence Kelley, Edith Abbott, and Sophonisba Breckenridge, and the emerging "helping professions" of social work, public nursing, school counseling, and teaching. Kelley's extraordinary career gives some sense of these connections. She concentrated her academic research on statistical studies of the health of women industrial workers and children; she worked as a specialist on these issues for the Illinois Bureau of Labor Statistics; she was an active participant in Jane Addams's Hull House; and she also was a vocal supporter of the National Child Labor Committee and the National Consumer League. The settlement house movement, the child labor movement, and the movement for Progressive educational reform were integrally linked both to the "helping professions" and to academic social science.[15]

Similar connections existed between the social sciences and the industrial labor movement. As Andrew Ffeiffer has shown in his *The Chicago Pragmatists and American Progressivism*, the pragmatist writings of John Dewey, James Tufts, and George Herbert Mead were shaped by their involvements in and experiences of Chicago labor struggles in the wake of the contentious and bloody Pullman strike of 1894 and by their participation in the movements for industrial arbitration, housing, and zoning reform in Chicago that emerged in response to these conflicts.[16] In the 1890s the University of Chicago was the center of a new approach to the empirical investigation of urban and labor conditions, pioneered by the sociology department under the leadership of Albion Small and Charles Henderson. Much of this work was inspired by the *Hull House Maps and Papers* (1895), an empirical study conducted under the leadership of Jane Addams and Florence Kelley, and also by empirical research, supported by the Chicago School of Civics and Philanthropy, undertaken by Julia Lathrop of Hull House in collaboration with Sophonisba Breckenridge and Edith Abbott.[17]

While the network of Progressive public intellectuals and teachers, empirical researchers, and activists was especially dense and influential in turn-of-the-century Chicago, similar networks were established in other cities centered around other universities. Perhaps the most para-digmatic, and politically influential, was the nexus of scholars, activists, and politicians centered around John R. Commons of the University of Wisconsin in Madison. Inspired by the social democratic theories of economists Henry Carter Adams and Richard T. Ely, Commons virtu-ally created the academic field of labor history. Through a series of con-tract research assignments—with the Democratic National Committee, the Industrial Commission of 1900, the famed Pittsburgh survey of 1907–1909, and the National Civic Federation—Commons worked tire-lessly as a public researcher and intellectual with close ties to Progres-sive reformers in the state house in Madison and the U.S. Capitol in Washington. As Leon Fink has observed: "combining research on labor history, industrial relations, and economic theory with an active concern for public policy, Commons and his students at Madison contributed significantly to the Progressive political thrust of the state in the La Fol-lette years and beyond. In addition to the industrial relations field, such areas as civil service law, utility regulation, workmen's compensation (as it was then known), and later unemployment and monetary policy all received sustained, creative attention from the 'Wisconsin crowd.'"[18]

In his seminal book *Progressive Intellectuals and the Dilemmas of Demo-cratic Commitment*, Fink argues that the possibilities—and limits—of such intellectual engagement were epitomized by the Commission on Indus-trial Relations established by President Woodrow Wilson in 1912 and chaired by Frank P. Walsh, a Kansas City attorney and labor reformer. The Commission has been the subject of much discussion in the historical lit-erature, much of it focused on its close connection to business elites and its "corporate liberal" antipathy to class conflict.[19] The Commission clearly was tied to business elites, and it sought to stabilize an unstable situation characterized by a wave of strike violence that broke out throughout the nation in 1911. Nonetheless, whatever its conservatism or its limitations, the Commission was an extraordinary phenomenon in its own time, and an instructive one to consider from the vantage point of our own time, in which it is hard to imagine such a serious body being even convened. Precipitated in part by a petition signed by a group of re-formers that included Jane Addams, Lillian Wald, Rabbi Stephen Wise, and the Reverends Howard Melish and John Haynes Holmes, the Com-mission sought to investigate the causes of class conflict and to propose public policy responses to it. In the words of the petitioners: "Today as fifty years ago, a house divided against itself cannot stand. We have to solve the problems of democracy in its industrial relationships and to solve them along democratic lines."[20]

The Commission was a corporatist body consisting of representatives of business, labor, and government. Its staff was directed by Charles Mc-

Carthy, a student of Commons, and included Selig Perlman, William Morriss Lieserson, and other Commons students and associates. "Political freedom," its Final Report stated, "can exist only where there is industrial freedom; political democracy only where there is industrial democracy." The Report put forth a series of social democratic proposals that included legislation to protect the right of labor to organize and to enable the prosecution of employers who abridge this right; a recommendation that the Bureau of Labor Statistics gather and publish data on wages and working hours; and legislation to secure an eight-hour day, to protect child labor, to equalize the pay between the sexes, and to provide federal sickness insurance.[21] In many ways the Report anticipated the most advanced New Deal social legislation, and in one respect this underscores the weakness of the Commission, whose proposals were unrealizable in their own time. But most notable for my purposes is the extent to which it represented the realization of a Progressive conception of the relationship between knowledge and social advancement. And if the most social democratic of the Commission reforms were not implemented, it is nonetheless the case that in its investigatory and deliberative capacity the Commission played an important role as an agent of public enlightenment and of corporate regulation. Further, its proposals reflected, and gave public legitimacy to, similar measures that were being implemented at the state and local levels. As Fink sums up this period "[it] offers ample testimony to the quality of labor-oriented engagement by a generation of socially conscious intellectuals. Whether by joining in forums with labor leaders and social reformers, establishing professional associations through which to maximize their influence on public opinion, or training a new generation of citizens and scholars, the new school economists etched in the possibility of a formal intellectual counterpart to labor-populist currents in workplaces and electoral politics. Perhaps most significant, these intellectuals imagined that the 'scientific' development of their own field of knowledge was intimately bound up with the welfare of working people."[22]

Such social scientific engagements were not, to be sure, "radical." While many of these intellectuals worked in the orbit of socialist politics, most of them were committed to an emphatically meliorist conception of social inquiry and public deliberation, and an incrementalist understanding of social change; and they saw their interventions as exercising a moderating influence upon social conflict by promoting cooperative and "pragmatic" rather than "absolutist" approaches to the solution of social problems. As Dewey and Tufts put it in their influential *Ethics*, published in 1908: "The need of the hour seems . . . to be the application of methods of more deliberate analysis and experiment. The extreme conservative may deprecate any scrutiny of the present order; the ardent radical may be impatient of the critical and seemingly tardy processes of the investigator; but those who have considered well the conquest which man is making of the world of nature cannot forbear the conviction that the cruder method of trial and error and the time-honored method of prejudice and partisan controversy need not longer dominate the regulation of life and society. They hope for a larger application of the scientific method to the problems of human welfare and progress."[23] Progressive intellectuals exemplified what C. Wright Mills called "liberal practicality," a broadly functionalist approach to the reequilibration of social life, and a political orientation supporting "deliberate," piecemeal reform rather than revolutionary upheaval.[24] This does not mean that they were simply dyed-in-the-wool partisans of technocratic social engineering and control, however much they later came to be seen in this way by supporters and critics alike. Progressive intellectuals promoted a creative and thoroughly reformist agenda based on the regeneration of democratic publics and the social democratization of public policy. While there were tensions to be sure between their democratic inclinations and their emerging professional allegiances, Progressive intellectuals were able to navigate these tensions in a way that avoided the elitism and insularity that later came to characterize academic life. Progressive intellectuals wrote for periodicals and magazines that reached a broad reading public; they worked closely with social movements and with reformist politicians; and they undertook research that was relevant to the concerns of these movements and movement-politicians.

Here too, as with liberal Protestantism, the contrast with intellectual life today could not be more stark. It is of course hard to generalize about such a diverse and complex set of institutions as the contemporary American academy. Indeed, its very complexity is a symbol of the academy's distance from its earlier history; if the American academy at turn of the century was a dynamic, expanding social universe, run by entrepreneurial leaders with a sense of liberal vision, today's academy is a lumbering beast, a mammoth complex of routinized, bureaucratic, and conservative institutions and predispositions.

Such institutions, whatever else they may claim, house no current analogue to the "Progressive intellectuals." There are, to be sure, academics who identify with broadly Progressive aspirations, many of them involved in current efforts to resuscitate Progressivism. But such figures tend to be disciplinary outliers, lacking in the broad institutional support and political connections possessed by their Progressive forbears. Some may be genuine academic "stars," and they may have access to research funds and may even run their own "centers." But these "progressive" efforts are not at the heart of the university, and they do not hold the interest of the vast majority of faculty, graduate students, or administrators.

There are, to be sure, "research institutes" almost beyond number, pursuing empirical research based on the most advanced social scientific approaches and theories. But, as C. Wright Mills pointed out almost half a century ago, such institutes tend to practice an "abstracted empiricism" that is devoid of any broad vision or practical idealism. A simple perusal of the core professional journals—the *American Journal of Sociology*, the *American Economic Review*, the *American Political Science Review*—confirms this picture. These texts promote a highly professionalized and indeed esoteric research agenda. Based on the most up-to-date forms of statistical analysis and mathematical modeling, these journals typically are barely readable in ordinary English. Far from the model of "civic professionalism," the contemporary social sciences gravitate toward a narrow and self-referential form of intellectual practice. A cynic would contend that in this universe what matters is not relevant knowledge but citation indexes, vitae expansion, and career advancement. A less jaded commentator would simply observe that what passes for important or relevant "knowledge" is highly removed from considerations of broad public consequence. Indeed, the very standard of "broad public consequence" is cast under a cloud of suspicion by social scientists well-trained in the hallowed canons of "value-freedom" and committed above all to "research productivity" based on peer review, i.e., based on the judgments of other professionalized academicians who speak a specialized and virtually private language. This is not to say that all such research is meaningless or irrelevant. It is simply to observe that the question of relevance is not one that is taken seriously.

The mainstream social sciences thus lack the practical idealism, bordering on missionary zeal, that energized Progressive intellectuals and helped to propel their ideas into the public domain. Beyond the general torpor and insularity of social scientific inquiry is the fact that the prevalent theoretical approaches are diametrically opposed to the general principle of Progressive social science, the principle of intelligent public purposiveness. The fields of economics, sociology, and political science are increasingly dominated by rational choice paradigms that share in common a commitment both to methodological individualism and to the idea that self-interested when not self-*maximizing* behavior is the basic inalterable principle of social life. Rational choice is obviously a broad rubric, and much could be said about its methodological sophistication, its internal complexity, and both its scholarly accomplishments and its theoretical deficiencies.[25] But my point here is a simple one—there is an obvious correspondence between rational choice approaches and the generally antistatist and privatizing tendencies in the broader public domain. Far from resisting these tendencies, rational choice confirms them by calling into question the very idea of "public good," "public intelligence," or "public action." Indeed, a complete account of the rise of its ascendancy, and of its connection to other antistatist and neoliberal approaches in the social sciences and in policy debates, would also have to consider the role of conservative think-tanks such as the Heritage Foundation and the American Enterprise Institute, which have worked with great financial resources and even greater ingenuity to delegitimize holistic liberal approaches and to promote free market approaches to social inquiry. It is hard to imagine an approach farther removed from the Progressivism of Richard Ely, John Commons, or Herbert Croly than rational choice, unless it is conservative Christian fundamentalism, which does for scientific relevance and public intelligence in the religious sphere what rational choice does in the academic.

There is one major exception to this schematic characterization of academic life—the development of cultural and identity-centered approaches in social theory, centered mainly in sociology and anthropology, and even more so in "area studies" programs such as Women's Studies, Gender Studies, and Cultural Studies, that are heavily influenced by antiscientific and literary-critical theories. Here too there is much to be said about these approaches. In the broadest of terms they are related to the explosion of identity politics of the 1960s, and partake both of the strengths and weaknesses of this politics, of which more below. But in terms of the general contrast that I wish to draw, the point should be painfully obvious: ironically, while diametrically opposed to rational choice in tonality, these approaches share with rational choice approaches a suspicion of the discourse of public good, and likewise dismiss the idea of an engaged and relevant social science that might promote "progressive" public policy. When engaged—and I say "when" deliberately, because these intellectual practices can be as esoteric and insulated as the most mathematized social science—these cultural approaches tend to avoid precisely the kinds of institutional and public policy concerns that were at the heart of Progressive intellectualism and that would have to be at the heart of any serious revival of Progressivism today.[26]

The absence of an integrated and purposive vision of social science is something that has not gone unnoticed by neoprogressives. Michael Piore, for example, has insisted that a current revival of Progressivism "would require first a breakthrough in the social sciences that would clarify the underlying constraints upon policy" and would project a compelling vision of institutional reform.[27] Piore is correct. Without such an intellectual "breakthrough," it is hard to see how Progressivism can be projected, either among policy analysts or among the broader public, as a compelling or hegemonic conception of government. We may recall Herbert Croly's observation of 1914: "A movement of public opinion, which believes itself to be and calls itself essentially progressive, has become the dominant formative influence in American public life."[28] Only on the basis of a rejuvenated, confident, and institutionally dynamic Progressive social scientific movement is such a "movement of public opinion" likely to occur. And yet while this may be true as a functional proposition, it does not follow from this that such an intellectual rejuvenation is likely to occur. Indeed, the current state of academia gives little cause for succor, and is simply another reason to consider the revival of Progressivism to be no more than a remote possibility. For as Mary Furner has written:

> It should perhaps be observed from the perspective of the late twentieth century, when the era in which politics and policy were conducted within the framework provided by the new liberalism has ended, that intellectuals who constructed its major variants were an especially privileged and at the same time responsible breed, deserving of a special claim on our attention . . . unlike many of those engaged in reinventing government and downsizing welfare today, they assumed that society as a whole somehow bore collective responsibility for the welfare of its members, and that purposeful action, through enlightened voluntary cooperation among responsible groups in civil society or through the auspices of government, could bring about desirable results. The post-new liberal era of "rational choice," resurgent laissez-faire, talk of market solutions for problems ranging from teen pregnancy to environmental pollution . . . is a very different time indeed.[29]

THE RISE AND FALL OF CLASS POLITICS

Progressivism represented a response to the emergent problems of a modern industrial capitalist economy. But "social problems" do not define themselves, nor do they call forth their own solutions. And among those factors fueling Progressive reform, none were more important than the prevalence of class politics in turn-of-the-century American society.

Much has been written about the "corporate liberalism" of the Progressive era. Historians such as James Weinstein, Gabriel Kolko, and Jeffrey Lustig have argued that the national administrative state, with its corporate regulation and its meliorist social policy, was largely designed by, and served the interests of, the emerging class of corporate capitalists. There can be no doubt that, as Martin Sklar has shown, such policies as unemployment and workmen's compensation and the Federal Trade Act served the interests of corporate capital, underwriting the rationalization of business, absorbing the third party costs of private transactions, and legitimating the new form of capitalism through Progressive notions of "public interest." There was a clear functional correspondence between Progressive liberalism and the new requirements of large-scale industrial capital accumulation. The old political regime, resting on decentralized authority, partisan corruption, and common law, was inconsistent with the new form of national capitalism. But even Sklar acknowledges that "corporate liberalism emerged not as the ideology of any one class, let alone the corporate sector of the capitalist class, but rather as the cross-class ideology expressing the interrelations of corporate capitalists, political leaders, intellectuals, proprietary capitalists, professionals and reformers, workers and trade-union leaders, populists, and socialists."[30]

As Sklar's comment indicates, working-class politics exerted a powerful influence during the Progressive era. American society from the outset had been shaped by a "producerist" ethos that accorded moral as well as economic priority to independent laboring activity.[31] The rise of the factory system and of corporate forms of economic activity challenged this ethos by compromising the independence of laborers, expropriating their knowledge and skills, and enveloping them in a vast socioeconomic network over which they had little control. Workers and farmers responded to this challenge through forms of collective and sometimes militant action. But these responses remained profoundly colored by the ethos of producerism, and were supported by a dense network of working-class cultural practices and institutions. As an entire generation of labor and social historians has documented, working-class communities during this period possessed a high degree of "organic solidarity"; workers shared not only common economic circumstances but religious traditions, forms of leisure, civic connections, and a strong sense of place.[32]

As a result of this solidarity, the much vaunted "collective action problems" emphasized by contemporary rational choice theorists were easily supplanted, and the Progressive era was a period of sustained labor organization, solidarity, and struggle. During this period the Knights of Labor grew into a mass movement of upward of a million artisans and industrial workers, only to recede and eventually fade in the face of violent labor conflict; the American Federation of Labor spearheaded the coordination and expansion of craft unionism in America; and the industrial union movement, which would only come of age during the New Deal period, experienced its (often violent and protracted) birth-pangs. This period surely represented the ascendancy of working-class politics if not "the forward march of labor"; American society underwent a succession of waves of boycotts, strikes, factory occupations, and violent confrontations between labor and the forces of capital. Such events as the Homestead steel strike of 1892, the Pullman railroad strike of 1894, the Triangle Shirtwaist Factory fire of 1911, and the Lawrence textile strike of 1912 assumed a symbolic significance that far exceeded their substantial practical import, highlighting the pervasiveness of class conflict and serving as virtual calls-to-arms of the labor movement. As a result, millions of workers were drawn behind the banners of "labor."[33]

Beyond this industrial conflict, the Progressive era was perhaps the most prolific period in the history of the American left. The People's Party, the Industrial Workers of the World, the Debsian Socialists—these were powerful political movements that generated a rich culture of public debate and political opposition. Daniel Bell has termed the period 1900–1912 "the golden age of American socialism." It was a time when working class *political* radicalism was a pervasive force in society and in the culture at large. Books such as Edward Bellamy's *Looking Backward* and Upton Sinclair's *The Jungle* were best sellers. Bell reports that there was a flourishing socialist press, including 8 foreign-language daily newspapers, 5 English dailies, 262 English weekly newspapers, and 36 foreign-language weeklies. And James Weinstein reports that by 1912 the largest socialist weekly, *The Appeal to Reason*, had reached a circulation of over 700,000 per week. Socialist mayors were elected in Burlington, Vermont; Schenectady, New York; Milwaukee, Wisconsin; and numerous smaller cities; and in 1910 Victor Berger of Milwaukee was elected as the first Socialist Congressman in American history. In May 1912 the national secretary of the Socialist Party reported a total of 1,039 socialists holding elective public office, including 56 mayors, 160 councilmen, and 145 aldermen. Eugene Debs's garnering of over 900,000 votes in the 1912 presidential election represented merely the tip of the iceberg of this political radicalism.[34]

As I have already indicated, Progressive politics was in large measure an effort to coopt this political radicalism and to forestall its coming to power. This strategy of cooptation is pervasive in the literature of the period, from the Dewey and Tufts *Ethics* volume quoted above, to Croly's foreboding warnings about industrial conflict in *The Promise of American Life*. But perhaps the clearest expression of it can be found in Theodore Roosevelt's famous "New Nationalism" speech of 1909. Roosevelt, speaking in a way it is impossible to imagine any current American politician speaking, insists upon a new understanding of "the relations of property to human welfare" in the face of large-scale industrial combination and production. He calls for the right to regulate the uses of wealth and the terms and conditions of labor; for workmen's compensation; for state and national laws to regulate female and child labor; and for health and safety regulation of workplaces. And he explicitly issues this call against those "advocates of the rights of property as against the rights of men [who] have been pushing their claims too far." But he also makes clear that it is necessary to do this because "excess of every kind is followed by reaction," because he believes that the "excesses" of unregulated capitalism will generate massive discontent and will thus jeopardize private property itself. For this reason his "new nationalism" stands "against violence and injustice and lawlessness by wage workers just as against lawless cunning and greed and selfish arrogance of employers."[35] Behind Roosevelt's reformist call to arms is the frequent invocation of the danger of "lawless mob violence" on the part of workers, a clear reference to factory occupations, wildcat strikes, and revolutionary socialist agitation. Progressive liberalism was fueled by this fear of class conflict, a fear that was perhaps the most important precipitant of Progressive reform.

It is quite obvious that such highly politicized class conflict has utterly faded from the scene. Social classes no doubt still exist, though in highly complex and mediated ways, as even the most sophisticated forms of Marxist scholarship would attest; and struggles between capital and labor, including bitter and protracted industrial conflicts—the Staley strike, the UPS strike—continue to emerge, as is inevitable in a capitalist society. But such class identities and class conflicts have simply lost their broad political valence. The rhetoric of class, even the muted rhetoric central to Roosevelt's speech, has virtually evaporated. Industrial strikes may generate public sympathy and support, and surely may produce union victories—and defeats—but they typically are discrete, localized events that lack broad public resonance. And the union movement, in its dynamic, growing phases during the Progressive era, has dramatically declined, in terms of numbers—approximately 10 percent of the workforce is currently unionized—in terms of public status or political influence, and in terms of cultural cache. Again, I am not sounding the death knell of unionism. Unions continue to exist, to bargain collectively on behalf of their members, and to exert political influence; indeed Clinton's presidential victories, and the turnaround in the 1998 congressional elections, would have been inconceivable without strong union backing of the Democratic party. Yet, as Wade Rathke and Joel Rogers—two partisans of labor's revival—put it: "Labor's power in the economy is drastically diminished—with private sector union membership now down to the pre-New Deal level of only 10 percent, and strikes at their lowest level in fifty years. And it still hasn't figured out how to organize in today's political economy. Just to maintain its present share of the workforce, labor needs three hundred thousand new members a year; to bump present levels up one point—and labor is down twenty points from its 1950s levels—its needs a million a year. But nobody's seen anything like those numbers since the 1930's, and today's world is different."[36]

Today's world *is* different, dramatically different; that is the central point of my argument. The reasons for labor's decline are numerous: the political-economic success of the post-World War II social contract that, in tandem with the Cold War conformity and the delegitimation and repression of the American left, took the steam out of the labor ascendancy of the 1930s and led to the rise of a politically conservative, corporate union movement and a conservative working class as well; the growth of consumerism among the working class that, particularly in an age of television and consumer debt, has served to seriously weaken "producerist" identities and to suffocate other forms of cultural experience that in the past fueled the labor movement; the suburbanization of America, and the corresponding replacement of neighborhood culture by mall culture; and the rise of new social movements that have in many ways contested, transversed, and supplanted class politics.[37]

But surely as important as these profound historical and sociological developments is the shift from an industrial to a "postindustrial" economy, in which regular, full-time employment has given way to flexible accumulation, market volatility, corporate downsizing and other forms of restructuring. In this increasingly "post-Fordist" economy, two of the material foundations of industrial union organization—a stable employment base and standardized forms of mass production located in relatively fixed and stable geographical locations—are diminishing in significance.[38] These political-economic transformations have had profound social-psychological effects. As Richard Sennett argues in his book *The Corrosion of Character: The Personal Character of Work in the New Capitalism*, the new modes of flexible accumulation have engendered new ways of organizing work time, new ways of organizing one's work life and thus new ways of organizing one's life. This change is summed up, Sennett, argues, in the motto "no long term." And a society that offers fewer and fewer certainties, fewer long-term horizons, he argues, is a society that offers fewer opportunities for the development of a continuous and rooted personal character. The social world of flexible capitalism is a world of little that is enduring. It is a world of mobility and distrust. In such a world relationships can be improvised. But increasingly such relationships are fleeting, temporary, and contingent. In such a world the organic solidarities that sustained the labor movement of the past are being eviscerated.

This is a major theme of some of the most important work being done in contemporary sociology.[39] But its full measure has not been taken by those hopeful about a Progressive revival. For, despite the revival of the AFL-CIO under John Sweeney, despite genuine victories in organizing low-wage workers, sweatshop workers, etc., and despite the media attention focused on the anti-WTO protests in Seattle and elsewhere, the simple fact is that the social conditions of a mass labor movement no longer exist. This it not to say that workers don't matter politically. But it is to say that they matter less, and that the way they matter has changed. Ruy Teixeira and Joel Rogers are correct to argue, in their book *America's Forgotten Majority: Why the White Working Class Matters*, that most Americans are workers of some kind, that as workers they care about their standards of living and about their economic insecurities, and that these cares matter politically and might matter more politically.[40] But they are wrong to argue that the working class matters as the potential foundation of a new progressive majority in American politics. Members of the working class may hold certain opinions favorable to progressivism (and also some opinions unfavorable to progressivism, as Teixeira and Rogers concede but do not dwell on). But these individuals, however they may function as respondents of public opinion polls, are not organized as a class either culturally or politically and, because they are not organized as a class, they are unable effectively and collectively to articulate the concerns documented by Teixeira and Rogers, nor are they able to alter a party system that is hostile toward these "progressive" concerns. Given the sociological tendencies noted above, there is little reason to believe that this situation is likely to change.

In such an environment class-based forms of political conflict will continue to remain important. Indeed, as I argue in the next chapter, new forms of labor and class political initiatives—community-labor alliances, cross-border solidarity campaigns like the anti-Nike campaign—represent viable and important political innovations. But it seems clear that the "labor movement" as such, as a dynamic cultural and political formation capable of powerfully influencing public debate and public policy for much of the twentieth century, is in abeyance, and is unlikely to regain its historic stature. As Nick Salvatore put it in his superb essay "The Decline of Labor: A Grim Picture, A Few Proposals," "a structural transformation occurred over these last decades that undermines the hope that time is on 'our' side."[41] A dynamic, growing class-based politics, centered around unions and radical movements linked to unions, was a central impetus behind Progressive reform. And its current absence bodes ill for the revival of Progressive reform.

THE ECLIPSE OF THE PUBLIC 1:
THE TWILIGHT OF COMMON DREAMS

Coincident with the decline of class politics has been the extraordinary rise in the past thirty years of new lines of cleavage associated with what has come to be called "multiculturalism" or "identity politics." These cleavages are the result of the politicization of previously unorganized constituencies—women, homosexuals, racial minorities, environmentalists, and others—organized as "new social movements" contesting issues, relating to gender, sexuality, race, and ecology, that had historically been marginal to Progressive liberalism. There is a vast literature on these developments. That these movements are in important ways "new," and that they have transformed the American political landscape, is beyond question. Indeed, the impact of these developments in simultaneously fueling and weakening organized liberalism in the United States has become a virtual obsession of political writers trying to make sense of the unraveling of the liberal coalition in the 1960s and the rise of conservatism in the wake of this liberal unraveling.

Politics is always about perceptions of injury and visions of remedy, and about the formation of collective actors bound by common political perceptions and goals. In this sense politics is always about identity. What is novel, and consequential, about "identity politics" is the way in which new, previously unquestioned or repressed social agents have come to the fore, and have articulated new demands for recognition that exploded bedrock, "traditional" values taken for granted even by Progressive liberals, values like the naturalness of the patriarchal family and the predominance of the male breadwinner; the procreative functions of sexuality; the "pathological" character of nonheterosexual relations; the essentially WASP character of American national identity; and the objective and value-neutral character of nature as a source of "raw materials" to be exploited by an industrial, producerist society. How these values came to be questioned, and challenged, by the New Left movements of the sixties is beyond the scope of my argument. But that they *were* challenged is absolutely central to my argument about the current impoverishment of progressivism. For the mobilization of these constituencies, and the articulation of their issues—affirmative action; busing; abortion rights; equal pay for equal work; gay rights; environmental regulation—served to transform American Progressive liberalism. In the course of the sixties American liberalism came increasingly to be associated with these new constituencies and issues. A new, "postmaterialist" liberalism came into being, making the representation of previously underrepresented, marginalized and minority groups, and the use of public policy to "empower" these groups, central political priorities. In many ways this postmaterialist liberalism was both liberatory and successful, as American society underwent a seismic political and cultural shift in the direction of equality for African Americans, other racial minorities, women, and homosexuals, and in the direction of greater environmental consciousness and environmental regulation.[42]

But in other ways this very empowerment of the "new liberalism" profoundly and irremediably weakened the "old" Progressive liberalism. The immediate impact of this weakening was felt during the political crisis of the late sixties and early seventies, where escalating demands for racial justice and an end to the Vietnam War led to virtual civil war in the streets of America's major cities and to a serious breakdown of political authority. Hannah Arendt wrote of the *Crises of the Republic*. Arthur Schlesinger wrote of a *Crisis of Confidence*. The titles of major books on the period tell the story. *The War Within. Coming Apart. The*

Unraveling of America. In the words of James Miller, democracy was in the streets.[43] There was an explosion of democratic demands, for women's rights, civil rights, Black Power, gay rights, student rights. The result was what social scientists came to call a "governability crisis" of liberalism.[44] 1968 was the crucible. The year of the Tet Offensive and the Stonewall Rebellion, the year of the assassinations of Martin Luther King Jr. and Robert Kennedy, 1968 was also the year that George Wallace split the Democratic party on a platform of states rights and segregationism; and Richard Nixon won the White House and inaugurated a long period of Republic ascendancy in American national politics. The sixties were a period of liberalism and liberation, but also a period of liberalism's political implosion. The causes of this implosion were no doubt complicated, and it is beyond my purposes here to explore them. But the implosion itself served to permanently weaken liberalism and to undermine the political base of Progressivism. This weakening worked in two ways.

On the one hand what occurred was the balkanization of the political base of liberalism, the subject of Arthur Schlesinger Jr.'s 1991 *The Disuniting of America* and of Todd Gitlin's 1995 *The Twilight of Common Dreams.* Schlesinger, liberal stalwart, is overwrought about America's fixation with multiculturalism and heterogeneity and the recognition of difference, the consequence of which is the denial of national identity and national purpose. Gitlin, disappointed by the failure of the New Left to realize its most noble communitarian dreams, is disturbed by the culture wars that have "wracked" America, dividing university campuses, school boards, and neighborhoods and making the search for commonalities difficult if not impossible. The result of this balkanization is that economic inequality, urban poverty, and other pressing social problems persist, while multiculturalist intellectuals and activists argue about the meaning and political requisites of "identity" and American citizens argue about O. J. Simpson and Sister Souljah.[45] For Schlesinger and Gitlin, both the form and the substance of multicultural demands are fractious, for they are typically insistent, driven by a powerful sense of privileged victimhood, and presented in zero-sum terms that leave little room for negotiation and compromise. Are you for or against abortion? Are you for or against affirmative action or busing or Ebonics or the use of gay rights–friendly elementary school textbooks? The very way in which these issues tend to be posed exacerbates conflicts of opinion. And conflicts of opinion are then overinterpreted as reflections of being, as symptoms of white maleness or heterosexuality or skin privilege or the privileged standpoint of women or the special insight possessed by blacks. There is an inflationary logic to this that has been identified in numerous commentaries.[46] The result is not simply the balkanization of aggrieved identity groups—women, blacks, gays, etc.—or at least of important segments of these groups whose leaders derive authority from their claims to authenticity. Equally important is the alienation of these political forces from the more "traditional" and "mainstream" constituencies whose support has historically been central to the power of liberal Progressivism, most especially the blue-collar working class.

For if one result of the new identity politics has been a hyperinflation of multiculturalist demands, the other has been the powerful backlash against the multicultural agenda on the part of Middle America. This has been a major theme of post-Reagan political commentary. Books such as Thomas and Mary Edsall's *Chain Reaction*, Kevin Phillips's *Boiling Point*, E. J. Dionne's *Why Americans Hate Politics*, and Stanley Greenberg's *Middle Class Dreams* all make the same important point—that the "new liberalism" that emerged out of the New Left led to the rightward shift of the political base of the "old" liberalism. For many blue-collar workers and trade union members, the new liberalism ignored their own socioeconomic concerns in favor of a "cultural" politics of empowerment for marginalized groups. The racial and sexual politics of the new liberalism were particularly responsible for this backlash, as many whites came to see affirmative action, busing, and welfare itself as forms of racial favoritism that disturbed their neighborhoods and their "traditional" values, redistributing "their" precious tax dollars to the poor at their own expense; and as white males in particular came to see feminism and sexual liberation as assaults on the integrity of their authority within the family.[47] Beyond the growing resistance to new liberal social policy, these groups came to interpret new liberal critiques of the racism and chauvinism and narrow-mindedness of Middle America as an assault on and affront to their own self-image as hard-working and loyal Americans who did not experience the society as offering them any free rides. The story told by New Left activists about the American middle class was not a story that many members of the middle class recognized or felt comfortable with. The consequence was a deep well of bitterness and resentment toward this story and toward the political agenda based on this story.[48] Thus was born the phenomenon of "Reagan Democrats," and the rightward shift in public opinion increasingly mobilized around social and racial issues rather than class issues. This is the central theme of E. J. Dionne's acclaimed *Why Americans Hate Politics*—the "false polarization" around these symbolic and social issues at the expense of Progressive liberalism. The balkanization referred to above was thus not simply a fragmentation of "liberal" constituencies; it was also an escalating sense of conflict between these groups and more "traditional" groups; on both sides of the multicultural divide, there developed a tendency to treat the other as dogmatic, sectarian, and dangerous.[49] At the same time that the working-class base of liberalism was thus increasingly alienated, important sections of the liberal intelligentsia were equally estranged from the new liberalism, leading to the rise of neoconservatism that, now well institutionalized as a genuine conservatism, has come to exercise a strong influence on policy debates.[50]

Beyond this shift to the right of traditional "liberal" constituencies was the simultaneous ascendancy of the New Right itself, a dynamically and unabashedly *conservative* movement. As many commentators have noted, the New Right was a product of the sixties, an obverse of the cultural politics of the New Left. Reacting against the New Left and at the same time appropriating many New Left themes, the New Right emerged out of the conservative opposition to the desegregation and student radicalism of the mid-sixties and the George Wallace candidacies of 1968 and 1972. Like the New Left, the New Right denounced the "corporate liberalism" of liberal Progressivism, attacked "bureaucracy" and "the Washington elite" and "the establishment" and "big government," and articulated a conception of "authentic," "grass roots," and localistic democracy. But whereas the New Left articulated these themes in the name of empowering historically marginal groups, the New Right articulated these themes *in strident opposition to* such empowerment, in the name of empowering "the silent majority" of white Middle Americans, supposed adherents of "family values," partisans of normality.[51] In the 1980s this conservative New Right and neoconservatism achieved the synthesis that has guided public policy ever since, a synthesis dedicated to repudiating Progressivism and its "big government" and to curtailing if not dismantling both the social programs of the late sixties and early seventies and the very idea of a regulatory state at the heart of Progressive liberalism in this century.

The decline of political support for liberalism among the "middle classes," and the political shift of public opinion and public policy rightward, have been the two central facts of American political life of the past two decades. Bill Clinton, as candidate and as President, sought, with some success, to challenge this state of affairs, by adopting a "New Democratic" strategy of coopting and reappropriating neoconservative themes and explicitly appealing to the "middle-class dreams" of the middle-class, white majority. Clinton succeeded politically in staving off the tide of Republican electoral ascendancy and in reestablishing the Democratic Party as a player in national and presidential politics. But he did so at the cost of sacrificing the liberal commitment to a regulatory state and at the expense of the very identity of "liberalism" itself, as both the term and that which it has long signified have been avoided like the plague by New Democratic politicians.

Neoprogressive writers recognize the power of the new mobilization of bias against liberalism. They recognize that in the sixties political support for liberalism crashed in the manner of Humpty Dumpty, and that the task of a revived Progressivism is to put the pieces back together again. But they do not sufficiently reckon with the difficulty of accomplishing this task. This analytical failure takes two forms. On the one hand, there is a tendency to moralize about the new liberal preoccupation with identity politics and to call for a renewed commitment to transcending this in the name of a more expansive liberalism. Thus Dionne calls for an end to "false polarization" and to the adoption of a more conciliatory, pragmatic approach by liberals. And Gitlin calls for a renewal of "common dreams" of social progress and economic equality: "For too long, too many Americans have busied themselves digging trenches to fortify their cultural borders, lining their trenches with insulation. Enough bunkers! Enough of the perfection of differences! We ought to be building bridges!"

On the other hand, accompanying this plea for civility, dialogue, and a new communitarian liberalism is an argument about public receptiveness toward such a new liberal vision. Thus Dionne, Greenberg, and Teixeira and Rogers argue that what most Americans really want is such a liberalism, if only somebody would give it to them. What these writers argue, primarily on the basis of survey research, is that while the "supply side" of American politics has long failed liberalism, the "demand side" yearns for it. For when properly polled, Americans indicate that they are anxious about the society and the economy; and while they may be suspicious of "big government" or "the welfare state" in general, they actually support many public programs and desire an effective public policy that could help them deal with their fears about their futures and those of their children. As Teixeira and Rogers put it: "It's as if white working-class voters would like to be convinced that government could really do big things for them. They're just waiting for someone to make that argument, and that offer, in a compelling way. And the numbers tell us that any party that does so will dominate American politics in the future, with a popular base for a new and bolder approach to government."[52] This argument about public opinion is linked with an argument about the need for universalist and race-neutral social policies that have broad appeal.[53] If such policies are put up "for sale" on the political marketplace, it is argued, they would be bought up by an eager American public.

There are two problems with this belief that multicultural divisions can readily be transcended given the emergence of a sufficient political will to do so. The first is that it relies on a primitive form of populistic reasoning at odds with basic truths of political science. For, even assuming it to be the case that polls reveal a receptiveness to Progressive policy when questions are framed in a particular way, such a "public" is not a collective agent, and its "opinion" is essentially an artifact of survey methods. As political scientists have long known, what drives electoral politics and public policy is not amorphous "public opinion" but rather the organized and mobilized agendas of interest groups, political parties, and other elites who channel public opinion and direct it through the ways they frame the issues and the choices they make available. It is, in other words, the supply side, and not the demand side, that governs in American politics. Perhaps *if* an expanded liberal agenda were put forth it could garner much public support. But the existing organized interests and political parties are deeply invested in the current mobilization of bias and have demonstrated no inclination to putting forth such an agenda. There are good political reasons for this, in other words there are substantial *causal forces* at work that produce this result, among them the bureaucratic character of the parties and the distribution of money and power in the society. As important is the fact that while an expanded liberalism might be a successful platform, the current stasis also produces "success," for incumbents and for the two dominant parties.

And the reason why it does so is in part because public opinion itself is more complicated a phenomenon than the neoprogressives allow. Teixeira and Rogers are correct to reject a simplistic story about the essential racism and/or conservatism of many middle-class American voters. It may be the case that much racial resentment can be interpreted as resentment toward particular programs such as affirmative action, and that more universalistic programs might generate more support for liberalism. But it is also the case that these particular programs, and liberalism itself, have been symbolically constructed in racial terms for over thirty years. It may be possible to transcend this; doing so was indeed one of the achievements of Clinton (who accomplished this by following the neoprogressives's negative message without their positive message, supporting a "welfare reform" that repudiated the "new" liberalism without putting any substantial policy in its place). But it is also possible to exploit this racial symbolism. In other words, when political issues and identities are framed by politicians and activists in ways that foment racial symbolism and stereotyping, this works too. It works for conservatives in many parts of the country (from Tom DeLay in Texas to John Hostettler in Indiana) who continue to garner political support by condemning "big government" and "Washington liberals" with rhetoric reminiscent of George Wallace; and it works as well for many racial liberals (such as Maxine Waters in California) who are inclined, for example, to interpret any challenges to affirmative action or welfare as simple instances of racism. There are, in other words, strong forces, on the supply side but also on the demand side, supporting the current mobilization of bias against Progressive liberalism. If the political will to challenge this existed such a project might succeed in the long haul, assuming it were able gradually to build support and forestall backsliding in a political system weighted toward short-term calculation—a big assumption indeed. But this brings to mind the silly joke "if my grandmother had wheels, she'd be a bicycle." The problem is, such a will does *not* exist. And bringing it into existence under current conditions is a daunting undertaking, confronting enormous chicken and egg problems. Because for every positive incentive to the development of an expansive, universalistic liberalism, there exists a negative incentive, in the form of entrenched constituencies, rhetorics, and habits.

And this brings me to the second problem with the neoprogressive argument. Even when neoprogressives acknowledge the power of multicultural divisions and the need to transcend them through force of will, they tend to view such divisions as aberrations or unfortunate historical mistakes or diversions from the authentic path of liberal progressivism. If only, it is implied, activists would come to see that their multicultural fixations are counterproductive, and that they impede the progress of liberalism, and if only liberal politicians would stop "indulging" such activists. The problem here is that there exists no authentic path of liberal progressivism, and that in historical fact liberal progressivism has been, alas, a powerful and hegemonic movement but also a partial and limited one. Liberal progressivism *did* marginalize questions of gender, sexuality, race, and ecology. It did not organize on the basis of these concerns, nor did it often acknowledge the salience of these concerns. Liberal progressives, instead, made their peace with racism, sexism, homophobia, and environmental destruction. There are good historical reasons why this was so. There is no reason to interpret this in all cases as a sign of the essential moral turpitude of liberals or liberalism. But because it was so liberal progressivism was invested in a state of affairs that new social movements, once politicized, could not help but to contest. The ardent contestation, implosion, and fragmentation of liberal progressivism that took place in the sixties was thus no unfortunate mistake or excess. It was a necessary thing. In the name of social justice liberal progressivism deserved to be contested.[54] And the levels or mistrust and resentment that this contestation produced—on the part of activists pressing for social change and on the part of activists pressing to forestall social change—were equally necessary. They were the inevitable outcomes of a necessary change. Books such as Edsall and Edsall's *Chain Reaction* and Phillips's *Boiling Point* concede this by their very titles. What took place was a "natural reaction," a wholly explicable and indeed predictable consequence of the coming to the fore of grievances that could no longer be denied but that many Americans were not yet fully prepared to recognize.

In many ways, then, the implosion of Progressive liberalism in the sixties should be viewed as an expression of this liberalism's underlying limits, limits that had by then become increasingly clear. On the one hand it had historically failed to thematize a range of important issues. On the other hand both its temperament and its mode of historically incorporating grievances was bureaucratic and elitist. For these reasons, by the sixties organized liberalism became widely perceived as a merely aggregative liberalism—what Theodore Lowi called "interest group liberalism"—catering to well-connected interests but lacking any broad vision or participatory dimension and thus lacking democratic legitimacy.[55] The revolts of the sixties—first of the New Left, and then, in reaction, of the New Right—and the "culture wars" that have ensued can thus be seen as symptoms of the democratic deficit of a liberalism that had become increasingly alienated from its original impulses and energies.

I am not arguing that current multicultural divisions are thus beyond politics, essential antagonisms that can neither abate nor be redirected. I am not denying that these divisions might be given different form depending on how intellectuals construct them and political leaders politicize them. But I am insisting that these divisions are very real and very powerful, and that they cannot easily be transcended.[56] For they are part of the natural history of our time. Neoprogressives might wish them away, might issue eloquent appeals for their transcendence, and might envision noble policies designed to help cement the necessary bridges. But such an optimism of the will should be chastened by the requisite pessimism of the intellect. For a sober analysis reveals that this project confronts serious obstacles, particularly given the other obstacles to a progressive revival already noted. And particularly in a society dominated by a media culture that is not hospitable to moderation. It is to this final limit of neoprogressivism that I now turn.

THE ECLIPSE OF THE PUBLIC 2:
THE DECLINE OF THE PUBLIC SPHERE

Behind Progressivism, then, was an overlapping set of dynamic constituencies that converged to support a genuine Progressive hegemony—liberal Protestants, reformist academics, and working-class movements and parties. As important as these constituencies, however, were the communicative means that made possible their mobilization and political projection. Progressivism as a movement and an ideology of regulation and social control, was rationalist, committed to the idea of intelligent public responsiveness. Progressives viewed the state as the ultimate repository of social intelligence, and they viewed society as a dynamic source of opportunities and challenges that precipitated creative state responses. The theory and practice of Progressivism thus relied in important degree on the flourishing of a robust public sphere capable of both translating pri-

vate troubles into public issues, and of signaling state officials about social problems and latent political demands. Without communication there
could be no Progressivism. As Eldon Eisenach writes of Progressive organizations and institutions: "their internal energies and external ends
could not have been successfully projected into the larger social and political world without extensive networks of communication and publicity
independent of and often in opposition to existing centers of authority
and power."[57]

One source of this publicity was the media of the Christian social gospel
noted above—magazines, novels, and sermons, comprising both an oral
and a written culture of reformist moral exhortation. Another was the literature of the emerging social scientific disciplines, which sought to address matters of broad public consequences and to reach beyond narrow
parochial audiences. A third was the extensive working class and socialist media, also noted above, which, through innumerable daily, weekly,
and monthly publications, regularly purveyed political and economic critique in English and in a range of other European languages. Each of the
dynamic sectors of the society, then, had their own "public sphere," and
these spheres interacted and intersected and sought broad public cache at
a time when the very identity of the society and the state was in question.

Equally important was the growth of the national media, the expansion
of national newspapers and in particular the proliferation of "muckrak-
ing" publications dedicated in whole or part to exposing political and
economic corruption and to challenging official rationalizations for the
problems thrown up by industrialization, urbanization, and modernization more generally. Mass-market magazines such as *McClures*, *Ladies
Home Journal*, the *Saturday Evening Post*, *Century*, *Cosmopolitan*, *Munsey's
Magazine*, and *Scribners* developed circulations in the hundreds of thousands and in some cases millions; and they regularly carried accounts of
corporate and governmental malfeasance by writers such as Ida Tarbell,
Ray Stannard Baker, Lincoln Steffens, and Upton Sinclair. These exposes
had impact beyond the sheer number of their readers. In *Ministers of Reform*, Robert Crumden offers a fascinating account, for example, of the
role of Sinclair's book *The Jungle* in shaping public discourse leading to
the passage of the Food and Drug Act of 1906. The documentary and pho-
tojournalism of Jacob Riis and Lewis Hine similarly helped to frame a
growing public awareness of how, in the words of Riis's famous book, the
other half lived.[58] The Progressive era is often associated by scholars on
the left with the rise of technocracy, mass media techniques of manipulation, corporate advertising, and consumerism. This association is not mistaken, for these institutions were innovations of the period during which
Progressivism flourished. The Progressive era was an era of large-scale organization and the decline of small-town mores, informal networks, and

localism. It was an era of nationalization and nationalism, and along with the other changes noted earlier there developed for the first time a truly national media based on a mass-market audience. And for the period of Progressivism's ascendancy this media functioned largely as an impetus to Progressive reform. As Stewart Ewen has written: "At the end of the first decade of this century, the success of Progressive publicity was considerable . . . the enormous growth of reform-minded journalism and of its readership revealed the unprecedented power of the mass media as a tool for assembling the public nationally around a variety of social concerns. It was this public that brought a generation of Progressive politicians to office, locally and nationally, in the years between 1890 and 1914."[59]

Yet, as Ewen argues in his superb book *PR: A Social History of Spin*, the publicity of the Progressive era was "double-edged," for while Progressive journalists and editors were committed to Enlightenment ideals of public reason, political criticism, and especially the public importance factual truths hidden from view, "the stylistic ambience of these [Progressive] media and the besieged, anxious sensibilities of their readership began to alter the assumptions of that publicity. Here, in mass magazines and newspapers, an Enlightenment faith in the diffusion before the 'bar of public reason' was being shadowed closely by another, more modern media genre: sensational expose, tawdry tales of corporate greed, municipal depravity, and moral decay. A significant turn had been taken. For those of us who have been flooded by a cascade of 'tabloid television,' a now familiar media was in the process of being born."[60] At the same time that the content of Progressive media promoted moral outrage and social action, the forms of these media were beginning to generate a new culture of hyperbole, promotionalism and public relations associated with mass spectatorship and mass consumerism. This tendency was further intensified by World War I. On the one hand, the war generated a climate of conformity and repressiveness that helped to put an end to political radicalism and to the Progressive reformism that had been fueled by it. On the other, the war schooled American political elites in the possibilities for propaganda and mass dissimulation presented by the new media. George Creel, as Chairman of the Committee on Public Information, oversaw the development of an elaborate network of mass communication, deploying posters, billboards, and films to promote the war effort. As Ewen puts it: "the CPI was built around a conception of the mass media that had never before been applied. Looming over each individual division was a conception of the mass media that saw them as parts of an interwoven perceptual environment. It was the espoused goal of the CPI to impregnate the entire fabric of perception with the message of the war." The CPI served as a model for the development of what Ewen calls "new rhetorics of persuasion," based upon the abandonment of Enlightenment ideals of public rationality and their replacement by the idea that the "mass" was an inert aggregation amenable to marketing and to manipulation. As Ewen quotes the business analyst Roger Babson: "the war taught us the power of propaganda. Now when we have anything to sell the American people, we know how to sell it."[61] A new theory and practice of communication emerged, one that transformed the domains of commerce and politics.

In many ways the theorist and indeed the prophet of this development was none other than Walter Lippmann, the Progressive activist for whom the war betokened not the irrelevance of Progressive ideas of social intelligence and national purpose, but the need to embed these ideals in a new, more "realistic" understanding of social psychology and communication. In his books *Public Opinion* (1922) and *The Phantom Public* (1925), Lippmann argued that earlier Progressives had been the captives of a democratic naivete. Wedded to a Jeffersonian faith in the intellectual competence and civic responsibility of the ordinary individual citizen, they believed that an informed and spontaneously arising public opinion could be assured by a free press, and that "people are exclusively concerned with affairs of which the causes and effects all operate within the region they inhabit."[62] They believed, in other words, that public will formation was a fairly straightforward and unproblematic process, and that public reason was an emergent property of a free civil society.

Lippmann emphatically rejected these assumptions, and in these two books he made a powerful case for an alternative view: that public opinion is a shifting and manipulable artifact of the symbols, fictions, stereotypes, and simplifications projected by knowing economic and political elites. Ordinary citizens, according to Lippmann, possess neither the time, the inclination, nor the intellectual capacity to form intelligent and causally accurate understandings of their social world. Instead of being autonomous political agents, ordinary citizens are better viewed as the recipients of the images, claims, and policies of elites. While in making this argument Lippmann surely drew upon an arsenal of antidemocratic sentiments in the history of political thought, his argument was no mere reiteration of hackneyed elitist prejudices. For it was distinguished by its reliance on the most innovative and sophisticated theories of language and social psychology of his time. Lippmann's argument is essentially a *sociological* argument, about the complexity of the modern social world, the preoccupations with milieux characteristic of most modern inhabitants of such a world, and the development of new and more sophisticated theories of mass communication and means of mass communication. Together, these factors, according to Lippmann, render anachronistic the Jeffersonian or Kantian ideal of the rational and self-governing public.

Lippmann is the founder of the modern study of mass communications and the prophet of the modern practice of mass communications. While many, following John Dewey's brave *The Public and its Problems* (1927), have sought to challenge Lippmann's cynical view of the workings of public opinion and to hold out the possibility of a more authentic form of autonomous publicity, arguably none have succeeded in questioning the *factual accuracy* of Lippmann's prognosis. To put it more bluntly, while Lippmann surely was wrong to celebrate the new dispensation and to laud those empowered by it, there is little doubt that he correctly discerned its contours and its significance.[63] Indeed, I call him a prophet precisely because of the way that he anticipated developments that continue to unfold in our own time. For if Lippmann's prognosis was true of his own time, it seems even truer today, almost eighty years later. We have even less reason than did the Progressives writing in the wake of World War I for any optimism about the prospects for the flourishing of a truly critical and vigorous public sphere.

Indeed, of all the ways in which our own time differs from the moment of Progressive ascendancy, none is more important than this one. And the most egregious error of current neoprogressives is their failure to take account of this. Most neoprogressives subscribe to what I have earlier called a "rationalistic fallacy."[64] They believe that ordinary citizens perceive, if only dimly, the sources of their difficulty, and that they are disposed to think more deeply and more critically about these difficulties when properly engaged and informed. And they therefore believe that the active promotion of the truth about the causes of our problems will, in time, lead to progressive, forward-looking, remedial solutions based upon firm public support. This is a noble belief. Those of us sincerely committed to democratic values should wish that this were so, and should do what we can to help make it so. But we also must take full account of the way things really are and the reasons they are this way. This neoprogressives fail to do. Neoprogressives fail to take the full measure of the evisceration of public discourse, and the divorce of critical reason and effective political power, that are defining features of our age. These are no doubt enormously complicated issues, the topic of whole disciplines and paradigms, from media studies, rhetoric, semiotics, and cultural studies to political sociology, political psychology, and mass communications. It is far beyond the scope of my argument here to engage this topic in depth. But it is essential to point out the seriousness of this topic, and to observe that neoprogressives typically devote almost *no* attention to a discussion of the politics of communication, in spite of the fact that vigorous public debate and effective mass communication about neoprogressive issues and policies would seem to be a necessary condition of the success of their project.

For the sake of my argument here I would only briefly note some particularly important dimensions of the eclipse of public life whose significance seems to have eluded those hopeful about the revival of Progressive reform. The first, widely noted and extensively researched, is the extraordinary corporatization and concentration of ownership of the American mass media, which increasingly are owned, operated, and coordinated by a handful of multinational conglomerates such as Time-Warner/AOL, Murdoch News Corporation, and Bertelsman.[65] The second is the commodification of journalism and media that naturally and inevitably has accompanied this corporate media merger mania. It is not simply that increasingly public discourse is controlled by an ever smaller number of entities, diminishing the number of independent public voices. It is also that these voices increasingly have come to sound alike, as all become governed by the imperatives of consumerism and commercial success.

As so many commentators have observed, the media have increasingly become vehicles of "infotainment" rather than public information and education. This process has been abetted by new forms of corporate organization and new forms of mass communication, such as advertorials, infomercials, Court TV, "reality-based" television, docudramas, and the creation of veritable corporate "worlds"—associated with such corporations as MTV, Nickelodeon, and especially Disney—that blend news, entertainment, corporate advertising, and the licensing of spin-off merchandising. As Benjamin Barber has observed, these developments "blur the lines between domains once thought to be distinct," so that "the distinction between reality and virtual reality vanishes." As he writes: "distinctions of every kind are fudged: ABC places its news and sports departments under a single corporate division; television news magazines blend into entertainment programs, creating new teletabloids . . . films parade corporate logos (for a price), presidents play themselves in films . . . while dethroned governors (Cuomo and Richards) do Super Bowl commercials for snack foods in which they joke about their electoral defeat, Hollywood stars run for office . . . and television pundits become practicing politicians. Politicians can do no right, celebrities can do no wrong—homicide included. Nothing is quite what it seems."[66]

Barber's point, it is worth noting, regards the form of the mass media and the way it typically organizes experience. His point is not that the media favor a particular party line or ideological agenda. It is that they increasingly promote a cynical worldview in which meaningful distinctions are effaced and in which fleeting images are treated, by their producers and by their consumers, as essentially interchangeable and without real consequence. News items—the Clarence Thomas affair, the O. J. Simpson affair, the Clinton/Lewinsky scandal, the Clinton impeachment, the Elian Gonzales affair, the contested Bush-Gore election in Florida, the disappearance of Chandra Levy—become media events and media events become news items. Like fall fashions and John Travolta's film career, personalities, politicians, and public issues race before the public eye, become the subject of intense media and public obsession, and then disappear from view—without enduring consequence, perhaps to resurface later in a completely new guise as if the past did not exist, perhaps simply to fade into a back hole of historical forgetting. Today's obsession becomes tomorrow's irrelevance. Yesterday Bob Dole was a presidential candidate. Today he is a walking advertisement for the sale of Viagra. Tomorrow he appears in a soda commercial with a scantily clad teenage pop star parodying his own sexual prowess. Who are we watching? A public figure or an actor? What is the difference? Yesterday he was a partisan politician who seemed to incarnate real political values of consequence that some endorsed and others opposed. And this contest seemed to matter. Today he is simply an amiable personage, a television icon, whom we can all enjoy. Did those political values really make a difference to us anyway? Was the contest really real? Is this a question even worth thinking about?

As public distinctions become blurred, as controversies more and more take on the appearance of *staged* contests in which all will later be forgiven and forgotten, our society has become increasingly governed by what Stuart Ewen has called "all consuming images." Politicians and public issues become more and more like soft drinks ("image is nothing; thirst is everything" says the endless advertising campaign that seeks to convince us to buy Sprite instead of drinking water), replete with brand names and logos and empty promises of fleeting satisfaction. And citizens become more and more like consumers, recipients of targeted ad campaigns, who choose from the range of interchangeable products with full knowledge that tomorrow will bring new choices, that there will always be new images to consume and new goods to purchase, that nothing really is what it seems, and nothing has enduring value, and that none of this really matters anyway.[67]

Thomas Frank, in his book *The Conquest of Cool: Business Culture, Counterculture, and the Rise of Hip Consumerism*, presents a brilliant account of the way such cynicism has become the guiding ethos of mass advertising and of American consumerism. Mark Crispin Miller, in his *Boxed In: The Culture of TV*, has argued that TV, as a medium that promotes "endless irony," is the vehicle par excellence of this ethos of hip, knowing, cynical consumerism. Again, this is a complex subject, more complex than these brief comments and citations can possibly indicate. Nonetheless it is a subject of great importance, that cuts to the heart of neoprogressive hopefulness. For it calls into question the very possibility of a coherent public debate about the future of American politics and about the need for a Progressive alternative.[68]

My point is not that Americans are simply dazed or incapacitated by media-driven imagery. For Americans clearly are complicit in such a culture. They are active agents in the production of their own world. By and large, they are enthusiastic participants in the exercise of innumerable consumer choices, regarding the TV channels they watch and the Web sites they search and the stores in which they shop and the brands that they choose to purchase. The point is not a point about agency. It is a point about identity, and about the lack of seriousness with which the public world is treated by people whose identities are so profoundly shaped by a pervasive media culture of image-mongering in which they are caught up as consumers. Moreover, it is not that issues—pollution, taxes, jobs, schools—cease to matter in such a world, or that citizens have become utterly incapable of thinking or talking about such issues. It is that the means for meaningful public communication about such issues on a large scale have been eclipsed and replaced by means of communication profoundly inhospitable to such communication, media with other purposes and other effects. And it is that an ethos of cynicism about distinctions and boundaries and enduring commitments—and thus an ethos cynical about politics, which is all about distinctions, boundaries, and commitments—has come to prevail, and that in such a culture cultural critics and social reformers and Progressive activists confront profound and probably unsurpassable obstacles. For we live in what Jeffrey Scheuer has called a "sound bite society."[69] And while such a society is surely not without its pleasures, nor without its genuine freedoms, it is a society lacking the depth, the seriousness, and the communicative means of deep and systematic social criticism and political transformation.

NOTES

1. Steven Rockefeller, *John Dewey: Religious Faith and Democratic Humanism* (New York: Columbia University Press, 1991), p. 27.

2. Jean Bethke Elshtain, "God and Man in the Oval Office," *New Republic* (March 22, 1999), pp. 37–40.

3. David Danbom, *"The World of Hope": Progressives and the Struggle for an Ethical Public Life* (Philadelphia: Temple University Press, 1987), pp. 80–111.

4. Eldon Eisenach, *The Lost Promise of Progressivism* (Lawrence, KS: University Press of Kansas, 1994), p. 11.

5. Edward Alsworth Ross, *Sin and Society: An Analysis of Latter-Day Iniquity* (Boston: Houghton Mifflin, 1907).

6. Robert Westbrook, *John Dewey and American Democracy* (Ithaca, NY: Cornell University Press, 1991), p. 79.

7. See Robert M. Crunden, *Ministers of Reform: The Progressives' Achievement in American Civilization, 1889–1920* (New York: Basic Books, 1982); Eisenach, *The Lost Promise*, pp. 22–47.

8. On this theme, see Robert Wuthnow's "The Moral Minority: Where Have All the Protestants Gone?" *American Prospect* (May 22, 2000), pp. 31–33.

9. John F. Persinos, "Has the Christian Right Taken Over the Republican Party?" *Campaigns and Elections*, vol. 15, no. 9 (September 1994), pp. 20–24. See also James A. Barnes, "Rightward March?" *National Journal* (August 6, 1994), pp. 1847–51; W. John Moore, "The Lord's Litigators," *National Journal* (July 2, 1994), pp. 1560–65; and Matthew C. Moen, "From Revolution to Evolution: The Changing Nature of the Christian Right," *Sociology of Religion*, vol. 55, no. 3 (1994), pp. 345–57.

10. Jeffrey H. Birnbaum, "The Gospel According to Ralph," *Time*, vol. 5, no. 20 (May 15, 1995), pp. 28–36.

11. For nuanced overviews of the power of the Christian Right, see Mark J. Rozell and Clyde Wilcox, eds., *God at the Grass Roots: The Christian Right in the 1994 Elections* (Lanham, MD: Rowman & Littlefield, 1995), and Clyde Wilcox, *Onward Christian Soldiers?* (Boulder: Westview Press, 1996). On Dobson in particular, see Nancy Novosad, "The Right's New Messiah," *The Progressive* (December 22, 1996), pp. 22–26.

12. Hal Lindsay, *The Late, Great Planet Earth* (Grand Rapids: Zondervan, 1970); Pat Robertson, *New World Order* (Dallas: Word Publishing, 1991); and Tim LaHaye and Jerry B. Jenkins, *Left Behind: A Novel of the Earth's Last Days* (Thorndike, ME: Thorndike Press, 2000).

13. Quoted in Eisenach, *The Lost Promise of Progressivism*, pp. 139, 168.

14. See Harry Boyte and Nancy Kari, *Building America: The Democratic Promise of Public Work* (Philadelphia: Temple University Press, 1996).

15. See Kathryn Kish Sklar, *Florence Kelley and the Nation's Work: The Rise of Women's Political Culture, 1830–1900* (New Haven, CT: Yale University Press, 1995), and Ellen Fitzpatrick, *Endless Crusade: Women Social Scientists and Progressive Reform* (Oxford: Oxford University Press, 1990).

16. Andrew Ffeiffer, *The Chicago Pragmatists and American Progressivism* (Ithaca, NY: Cornell University Press, 1993).

17. See Dorothy Ross, *The Origins of American Social Science* (Cambridge: Cambridge University Press, 1991), pp. 224–26.

18. Leon Fink, *Progressive Intellectuals and the Paradox of Democratic Commitment* (Cambridge, MA: Harvard University Press, 1996), pp. 64–66.

19. See Gabriel Kolko, *The Triumph of Conservatism: A Reinterpretation of American History, 1900–1916* (New York: Free Press, 1963); James Weinstein, *The Corporate Ideal in the Liberal State, 1900–1918* (Boston: Beacon Press, 1968); Jeffrey Lustig, *Corporate Liberalism: The Origins of Modern American Political Theory, 1890–1920* (Berkeley: University of California Press, 1982); and Martin Sklar, *The Corporate Reconstruction of American Capitalism, 1890–1916* (Cambridge: Cambridge University Press, 1988).

20. Quoted in Weinstein, *The Corporate Ideal*, p. 182.

21. Quoted in Weinstein, *The Corporate Ideal*, pp. 191, 210–12.

22. Fink, *Progressive Intellectuals*, p. 61.

23. Quoted in White, *Social Thought in America* (London: Oxford University Press, 1976), p. 55.

24. C. Wright Mills, *The Sociological Imagination* (Oxford: Oxford University Press, 1959).

25. See Donald Green and Ian Shapiro, *Pathologies of Rational Choice Theory* (New Haven, CT: Yale University Press, 1994).

26. On this issue, see Russell Jacoby's *The End of Utopia: Politics and Culture in an Age of Apathy* (New York: Basic Books, 1999).

27. Michael Piore, *Beyond Individualism* (Cambridge, MA: Harvard University Press, 1995), p. 172.

28. Herbert Croly, *Progressive Democracy* (New York: Macmillan, 1914), pp. 1–2.

29. Mary O. Furner, "Social Scientists and the State: Constructing the Knowledge Base for Public Policy, 1880–1920," in Leon Fink, Stephen Leonhard, and Donald M. Reed, eds., *Intellectuals and Public Life: Between Radicalism and Reform* (Ithaca, NY: Cornell University Press, 1996), p. 181.

30. Martin Sklar, *The Corporate Reconstruction of American Capitalism, 1980–1916: The Market, the Law, and Politics* (Cambridge: Cambridge University Press, 1988), p. 35. Sklar goes on, however, to identify this coalition as all those "who could, to a greater or lesser extent, identify their outlook . . . with the rise, legitimation, and institutionalization of the corporate-capitalist order, and hence with the dominant position in the market of the corporate sector of the capitalist class."

31. See Christopher Lasch, *The True and Only Heaven* (New York: W. W. Norton, 1991), and Michael Kazin, *The Populist Persuasion* (New York: Basic Books, 1995).

32. On these themes, see the pioneering work of Herbert G. Gutman, especially *Work, Culture, and Society in Industrializing America* (New York: Vintage Books, 1976).

33. For an excellent overview, see American Social History Project, *Who Built America: Working People and the Nation's Economy, Politics, Culture and Society: Volume Two: From the Guilded Age to the Present* (New York: Pantheon Books, 1992), especially pp. 61–215.

34. See Daniel Bell, *Marxian Socialism in the United States* (Princeton, NJ: Princeton University Press, 1967), and James Weinstein, *Ambiguous Legacy: The Left in American Politics* (New York: New Viewpoints, 1975).

35. Theodore Roosevelt, "The New Nationalism," in *The New Nationalism* (New York: Outlook, 1910), especially pp. 23–25.

36. Wade Rathke and Joel Rogers, "A Strategy for Labor," *Dissent* (fall 1996), p. 78.

37. On consumerism, see especially Juliet B. Schor, *The Overspent American: Upscaling, Downshifting, and the New Consumer* (New York: Basic Books, 1998); James Medoff and Andrew Harless, *The Indebted Society: Anatomy of an Ongoing Disaster* (Boston: Little Brown, 1996); Stewert Ewen, *All Consuming Images: The Politics of Style in Contemporary Culture* (New York: Basic Books, 1988); and James B. Twitchell, *Lead Us into Temptation: The Triumph of American Materialism* (New York: Columbia University Press, 1999); on cultural impact of suburbanization, see Alan Ehrenhalt, *The Lost City* (New York: Basic Books, 1995); on the political impact of suburbanization, see Thomas Edsall and Mary Edsall, *Chain Reaction: The Impact of Race, Rights, and Taxes on American Politics* (New York: Norton, 1992), and Kevin Phillips, *Boiling Point: Democrats, Republicans, and the Decline of Middle-Class Prosperity* (New York: Harper, 1993).

38. See Bennett Harrison, *Lean and Mean: The Changing Landscape of Corporate Power in the Age of Flexibility* (New York: Basic Books, 1994); Lester Thurow, *The Future of Capitalism* (New York: William Morrow, 1996); Jeremy Rifkin, *The End of Work* (1993); and David Harvey, *The Condition of Postmodernity* (Cambridge: Basil Blackwell, 1989).

39. See Sennett's *The Corrosion of Character* (New York: W. W. Norton, 1998); Manuel Castells's *The Information Age: Economy, Society, and Culture: The Rise of Network Society* (Oxford: Blackwell, 1996); and Zygmunt Bauman's *Liquid Modernity* (Cambridge: Polity Press, 2000).

40. Ruy Teixeira and Joel Rogers, *America's Forgotten Majority: Why the White Working Class Still Matters* (New York: Basic Books, 2000).

41. Nick Salvatore, "The Decline of Labor: A Grim Picture, A Few Proposals," *Dissent* (winter 1992), pp. 86–87.

42. See Jeffrey M. Berry, *The New Liberalism: The Rising Power of Citizen Groups* (Washington, DC: Brookings, 1999).

43. Arthur M. Schlesinger Jr., *The Crisis of Confidence* (New York: Bantam, 1969); Hannah Arendt, *Crises of the Republic* (New York: Harcourt, 1972); Tom Wells, *The War Within: America's Battle over Vietnam* (Berkeley: University of California Press, 1994); Roger Rosenblatt, *Coming Apart: A Memoir of the Harvard Wars of 1968* (Boston: Little Brown, 1997); Allen J. Matusow, *The Unraveling of America: A History of Liberalism in the 1960's* (New York: Harper, 1984); and James Miller, *Democracy Is in the Streets* (New York: Simon and Schuster, 1987).

44. See, for example, Samuel P. Huntington's important "The Democratic Distemper," *Public Interest*, 41 (fall 1975), pp. 9–38.

45. Arthur M. Schlesinger Jr., *The Disuniting of America* (New York: Norton, 1992), and Todd Gitlin, *The Twilight of Common Dreams: Why America Is Wracked by Culture Wars* (New York: Metropolitan Books, 1995).

46. See, for example, Jean Elshtain, *Democracy on Trial* (New York: Basic Books, 1995).

47. Thomas Edsall and Mary Edsall, *Chain Reaction: The Impact of Race, Rights, and Taxes on American Politics* (New York: W. W. Norton, 1991); Kevin Phillips, *Boiling Point: Democrats, Republicans, and the Decline of Middle-Class Prosperity* (New York: Harper, 1993); E. J. Dionne Jr., *Why Americans Hate Politics* (New York: Touchstone, 1991); and Stanley Greenberg, *Middle Class Dreams* (New Haven, CT: Yale University Press, 1996).

48. See Jonathan Cobb and Richard Sennett, *The Hidden Injuries of Class* (New York: Knopf, 1972); Jonathan Reider, *Canarsie: The Jews and Italians of Brooklyn Against Liberalism* (Cambridge, MA: Harvard University Press, 1985); Christopher Lasch, "Right-Wing Populism and the Revolt Against Liberalism," in *The True and Only Heaven: Progress and Its Critics* (New York: W. W. Norton, 1991); Jim Sleeper, *The Closest of Strangers: Liberalism and the Politics of Race in New York* (New York: W. W. Norton, 1990); and William E. Connolly, "Fundamentalism in America," in *The Ethos of Pluralization* (Minneapolis: University of Minnesota Press, 1995).

49. Chris Bull and John Gallagher's book *Perfect Enemies: The Religious Right, the Gay Movement, and the Politics of the 1990's* (New York: Crown, 1996) is a brilliant account of this dynamic.

50. See Dionne, *Why Americans Hate Politics*, chapter 5.

51. See especially Alan Crawford's excellent *Thunder on the Right: The "New Right" and the Politics of Resentment* (New York: Pantheon, 1980).

52. Teixeira and Rogers, *America's Forgotten Majority*, p. xii.

53. See Theda Skocpol, "Sustainable Social Policy: Fighting Poverty Without Poverty Programs," *American Prospect* (summer 1990), pp. 58–70 and "The G.I. Bill and U.S. Social Policy: Past and Future," *Social Philosophy and Policy*, vol. 14, no. 2 (summer 1997), pp. 95–115; Paul M. Sniderman and Edward G. Carmines, *Reaching Beyond Race* (Cambridge, MA: Harvard University Press, 1997); Richard D. Kahlenberg, *The Remedy: Class, Race, and Affirmative Action* (New York: Basic Books, 1996); and William Julius Wilson, *The Bridge over the Racial Divide: Rising Inequality and Coalition Politics* (Berkeley: University of California Press, 1999).

54. This point is made brilliantly by Felicia A. Kornbluh in her essay "Political Arithmetic and Racial Division in the Democratic Party," *Social Policy* (spring 1996), pp. 49–61.

55. See Theodore Lowi, *The End of Liberalism* (New York: W. W. Norton, 1971).

56. See Benjamin DeMott, *The Trouble with Friendship: Why Americans Can't Think Straight About Race* (New Haven, CT: Yale University Press, 1998).

57. Eisenach, *Lost Promise of Progressivism*, p. 13.

58. See Hofstadter, *The Age of Reform* (New York: Knopf, 1955), pp. 186–93; Robert Morse Crunden, *Ministers of Reform: The Progressives' Achievement in American Civilization, 1889–1920* (New York: Basic Books, 1982), pp. 163–99; Daniel T. Rogers, *Atlantic Crossings: Social Politics in a Progressive Age* (Cambridge, MA: Belknap Press, 1998), pp. 149–60; Robert Westbrook, "Lewis Hine and the Two Faces of Progressive Photography," in Leon Fink, ed., *Major Problems in the Gilded Age and the Progressive Era* (Lexington, MA: D. C. Heath, 1993), pp. 320–29; and Russell Freedman, *Kids at Work: Lewis Hine and the Crusade Against Child Labor* (New York: Clarion, 1994).

59. Stuart Ewen, *PR: A Social History of Spin* (New York: Basic Books, 1996), p. 59.

60. Ewen, *PR*, p. 54.

61. Ewen, *PR*, pp. l, 116, 131.

62. Walter Lippmann, *Public Opinion* (New York: Harcourt, 1922), p. 269.

63. This is a point conceded by two of the most astute contemporary commentators on the intellectual history of this period. See James T. Kloppenberg, "Pragmatism: An Old Name for Some New Ways of Thinking," *Journal of American History*, vol. 83, no. 1 (June 1996), p. 134; and Robert Westbrook, "Democratic Evasions: Cornel West and the Politics of Pragmatism," *Praxis International*, vol. 13, no. 1 (April 1993), p. 10. It is also consistent with the argument of Jurgen Habermas's classic *The Structural Transformation of the Public Sphere* (Cambridge, MA: MIT Press, 1986).

64. See my "The Poverty of Progressivism," *Dissent* (fall 1996), pp. 43–44.

65. See Robert W. McChesney, *Rich Media, Poor Democracy: Communications Politics in Dubious Times* (New York: New Press, 2000) and Ben Bagdickian, *The Media Monopoly*, fourth edition (Boston: Beacon Press, 1992).

66. Benjamin R. Barber, *Jihad vs. McWorld* (New York: Times Books, 1995), pp. 84–85.

67. See Stuart Ewen, *All-Consuming Images: The Politics of Style in Contemporary America* (New York: Basic Books, 1988), and James B. Twitchell, *Lead Us into Temptation: The Triumph of American Materialism* (New York: Columbia University Press, 1999).

68. Thomas Frank, *The Conquest of Cool* (Chicago: University of Chicago Press, 1997), and Mark Crispin Miller, *Boxed In: The Culture of TV* (Evanston, IL: Northwestern University Press, 1988). See also *The Baffler*, the magazine of cultural criticism edited by Frank; and Mark Crispin Miller's more recent *The Bush Dyslexicon: Observations on a National Disorder* (New York: Norton, 2001).

69. Jeffrey Scheuer, *The Sound Bite Society: Television and the American Mind* (New York: Four Walls, Eight Windows, 1999).

4

+

Rethinking the Future of Democratic Innovation

The vision of a revitalized Progressivism is an anachronism. For while Progressivism offered a reformist agenda for a modernizing nation, we live in a postmodern age, in which the foundations of a regulatory politics have been eroded by a variety of centrifugal tendencies, and the forces of capitalist globalization have severely circumscribed the freedom of maneuver of the nation-state. These processes are a central theme of contemporary sociological theorists such as Manuel Castells, Ulrich Beck, Anthony Giddens, Antonio Negri, and Michael Hardt.[1] The sociologist Zygmunt Bauman has coined the phrase "liquid modernity" to summarize these new developments. If modernization was a process of constructing new, more grounded, foundational, "progressive," *solid* forms of human power—symbolized by industrial factories, mass political parties, and state bureaucracies—ours is a time of *liquification*, of the dissolution of enduring institutions, productive processes, and products. If modernity engendered forms of power based on the regulation of populations and social and economic processes within well-defined and territorially bounded spaces, "the prime technique of power is now escape, slippage, elision, and avoidance."[2] In such a society "sovereignties have become nominal, power anonymous, and its locus empty. If the traditional question 'What is to be done?' . . . is asked ever less frequently, and if when asked it tends to be quickly dismissed on the ground of a TINA (There Is No Alternative) creed, this is not so much for the lack of ideas as it is [for lack of] agencies which could conceivably carry them out. The assessment of the feasibility of actions and the practicality of projects is a function of the relative strength of the agent and its adversary; and under

117

present circumstances the main question . . . [for] which no clear answer is in sight, is the query 'Is anybody capable of doing whatever needs to be done?'"3

Of course such a picture runs the risk of caricature. Bauman does not mean that modernity has been thoroughly transcended. He does not mean that institutions no longer exist, that identities are utterly without endurance, or that forms of collective agency have completely disappeared. He means that institutions, identities, and agencies are in great flux and are continually being eroded, and that while social processes and routines surely persist, the means of collectively and authoritatively monitoring these processes and routines have dramatically diminished.

Bauman's broad sociological characterization is reinforced by the arguments of American political scientists such as Robert Putnam and Theda Skocpol, who have charted the recent dramatic decline in the United States of the kind of dense associational life capable of integrating ordinary citizens and generating progressive political commitments among large numbers of people.4 As Margaret Weir and Marshall Ganz sum up the conclusions of this literature:

> For most people, as political parties have ceased to be mass-based political organizations . . . politics has become simply another form of advertising, and a particularly noxious one at that. Interest groups flourish, but they too have lost much of their popular base, focusing instead on Washington-based, staff-led activities. Politics and policymaking have become unanchored, susceptible to pressures from more mobilized minorities on the right or foundering in search of some acceptable 'center.' But in a largely demobilized political context, the center has little organizational reality and, as a consequence, little dependable political force. . . . The so-called center has lurched toward the antigovernment right for lack of any meaningful grounding in the everyday experiences of most Americans, much less any strong counterpressure from progressive forces.5

For political as well as sociological reasons, then, the vision of some kind of Progressive assertion of mastery over the processes of social drift—to recall Lippmann's paradigmatic statement—has come to seem, and has come to *be*, lacking in credibility.

Assuming this to be the case—and the burden of the previous chapters has been to argue that it is—the question that arises is still the classic question, noted by Bauman: "What is to be done?" How, in other words, might some kind of collective agency or democratic regulation of society be undertaken under these new conditions? How might public means be mobilized in response to manifestly public problems? It is of course possible to embrace the new dispensation, and thus also to embrace the notion that there is simply nothing *to* do, that weighty political contention and innovative, remedial public policies are things of the past best relegated *to* the past. This is the position that today prevails across the spectrum of mainstream party-political thinking. The consensus among conservatives, neoconservatives, and neoliberals alike, is that the retraction of politics is a good thing. There is thus widespread celebration of the unhindered operation of third-wave technologies, global markets, and a so-called opportunity society centered on supposedly sovereign individual economic and philanthropic decisions. To join in this celebration is to treat the impoverishment of progressivism as a simple truism to be accepted.

But, as I have already indicated in chapter 1, such an embrace of the current dispensation is both credulous and heartless. It is credulous in its willingness to adopt the most Panglossian optimism about current social and economic trends, and to believe—in the face of much evidence to the contrary—that new forms of economic growth are universally advantageous and thus universally acclaimed, and that there exists a simple consensus on the beneficence of the present. And it is heartless in its disregard of the plight of the many whose own experiences of insecurity, marginalization, and anxiety about the future give the lie to such optimism. If neoprogressives are right about nothing else, they are surely correct to note the extent to which American society is plagued by many serious unsolved problems that demand public attention. The impoverishment of progressivism should thus not be a cause for celebration. It should be a cause for grave concern and serious inquiry. For if there exists no answer to the question about what is to be done, then we must consign ourselves to a world in which we have become the playthings of forces beyond our control. Such a world may bring some advantages, but it will also bring many risks and many costs, and these risks and costs, along with the benefits, will be distributed in ways that are both socially and morally arbitrary. In such a world there can be no serious commitment to justice. And in such a world there can be no meaningful practice of democracy. Even among mainstream political opinion, where such issues are rarely posed directly, there remains a gnawing sense that the current dispensation is deficient, that something more is required, in the way of policy but perhaps even more in the way of *legitimacy*, in order to solve public problems whose effects are undeniable.

The question that remains, then, is what *can* be done? How can some kind of politics of democratic problem solving and public regulation be constituted in the face of the erosion of support for Progressive liberalism and its "big government" forms of regulation? In what follows I sketch out an answer. I argue that the retrenchment of progressive politics is a veritable fact of life that can be and continues to be contested but cannot fully be turned back. For this reason it is on the terrain of civil society and its voluntary initiatives and third-sector organizations, and not on the terrain of the national state and its regulatory agencies, that the best chance for the revitalization of American democracy lies. This does not mean that civil society and the state can simplistically be counterposed, or that civil society initiatives can succeed without political support of various kinds. Civil society is surely no panacea, the enthusiasm of some of its partisans notwithstanding. It simply means that an ambitious agenda of political reform and socioeconomic regulation is unlikely to be enacted, and thus more modest and localized efforts represent the best hope for a left-liberal politics of democratic problem solving and public regulation.

Theorists of the so-called third way have correctly seen this. The third way represents a formula for electoral success but, more importantly, it represents a modest politics that embraces the terms of political "realism" and conducts itself on the terrain of political retrenchment. Third way politics, and the civil society–centered initiatives whose promotion is one of its hallmarks, has much to recommend itself under current historical conditions. But it is also a profoundly limited and unsatisfying form of politics. Partisans of the third way all too rarely acknowledge these limits. In failing to acknowledge them, they fall victim to their own form of Panglossian optimism. Instead, I argue, what is called for is an honest acknowledgment of the profound obstacles and tragic binds confronting left-liberal politics today, and a sober commitment to nourishing those efforts that promise, in limited ways to be sure, a modicum of justice and empowerment in the face of these obstacles.

HOW CIVIL SOCIETY INITIATIVES
OFFER AN ALTERNATIVE TO PROGRESSIVISM

In recent years a remarkably eclectic group of scholars, policy analysts, journalists, and activists from across the political spectrum have turned toward "civil society" as the answer to today's social problems. Refusing simply to celebrate the retrenchment of political agency in the face of market forces, most civil society advocates acknowledge that serious social problems do exist, and that meaningful forms of collective response are both necessary and possible. But, unlike neoprogressives, they maintain that such responses are best located in the sphere of civil society rather than in the sphere of conventional politics and public policy formation. The concept of civil society is notoriously fuzzy, containing many analytical and normative implications, and used in many different ways, so much so that many scholars have insisted that it should be jettisoned from serious discussion.[6] But it would be both mistaken and foolish to pursue this path. For the prevalence of the concept in scholarly and public discourse is important and revealing. It speaks to what Jürgen Habermas has called the "exhaustion of utopian energies" that had for a long time been invested in Progressive and social democratic forms of regulatory politics.[7] The turn to civil society in public discourse of the past two decades is no doubt a complex process. But there is also no doubt that it is in part an effort to locate a new site of practical idealism and democratic praxis.

While there is no simple consensus about civil society by those who invoke this concept, civil society typically is taken to denote that intermediate sphere standing between the state and the market, and between the modalities of sovereign political decision making on the one hand and individual self-interest on the other. Some civil society advocates, with roots in conservative and neoconservative critiques of the welfare state and its "therapeutic" culture, focus on such supposedly "moral" institutions as "the family" and religious congregations.[8] Others, closer to the left, are concerned primarily with the injustices of capitalist markets and focus on a broader range of voluntary associations, from non-profit organizations to community development corporations to trade unions and social movements.[9] There is no single civil society perspective or program, for one of the premises of the civil society discourse is the plurality of civil society associations and the inadequacy of political programs to express or represent this plurality. But there is nonetheless a general proposition common to writers and activists interested in the revival of civil society, and that is the view that neither the Progressive, regulatory state nor the free market is sufficient to the task of addressing America's social ills, and that the only way to address these ills is by strengthening civil society and its "mediating" institutions.

As their proponents argue, civil society initiatives and organizations have much to recommend them:

1. they work on the principle of subsidiarity, typically proposing to solve social problems at the lowest and most proximate level consistent with their solution. They thus tend to be localist in orientation, something that makes them appealing to all those, right and left, who are wary of the centralized, bureaucratic state and who seek to promote greater civic engagement through more localized and accessible forms of citizen participation;
2. they purport to promote individual and civic responsibility, requiring individual citizens to work collaboratively to achieve public goods whose benefits are transindividual. In this regard civil society initiatives can be seen as fostering empowerment rather than clientelism and dependence; deliberation rather than zero-sum strategic bargaining; and communitarian dispositions rather than predatory

practices aimed at colonizing public power on behalf of particular interests;

3. they purport to rest on social and civic self-organization, and on diverse forms of volunteerism, and they thus do not require that large amounts of money be allocated by the federal government.

Civil society initiatives thus appear to combine, at least ideal-typically, the virtues of entrepreneurial effort, efficiency, voluntarism, and civic-mindedness. For this reason they are often presented as being practical and effective in a way that welfare state regulations and allocations are not. Further, they are often seen as sources of "social capital" that build social trust and confidence in social and political institutions.[10] As Benjamin Barber sums up this general understanding of civil society: "[it] posits a third domain of civic engagement which is neither governmental nor strictly private yet shares the virtues of both. It offers a space for public work, civic business, and other common activities that are focused neither on profit not on a welfare bureaucracy's client services. It is also a communicative domain of civility, where political discourse is grounded in mutual respect and the search for common understanding even as it expresses differences and identity conflicts. It extols voluntarism but insists that voluntarism is the first step to citizenship, not just an exercise in private character building, philanthropy, or noblesse oblige."[11] There can be no doubt that the civil society idea has assumed great prominence in contemporary American political discourse. It is equally beyond doubt that corresponding to this discourse has been a proliferation of practical experiments often viewed under the rubric of civil society, and that such experiments have been promoted by an extensive and increasingly dense network of philanthropic foundations, academic institutions, and other organizations, including the Kettering Foundation, the Pew Charitable Trusts, the Bradley Foundation, the Open Society Institute, the National Civic League, The Hubert Humphrey Center at University of Minnesota and the Walt Whitman Center at Rutgers University. Carmen Sirianni and Lewis Friedland, in their important new book *Civic Innovation in America*, have gone so far as to call this collection of efforts a genuine "movement for civic renewal."[12]

The literature on civic renewal is enormous. It tends toward the descriptive, cataloguing the numerous and extraordinarily diverse attempts by citizen groups across the country and across the party-political spectrum to join together to solve public problems from urban blight to environmental degradation to economic insecurity to multicultural antagonism.[13] Such an idiographic and narrative approach has its limits. As I argue below, it often downplays the practical and political weaknesses of the efforts it catalogues. Indeed, the project of documenting civic effort, often drawing extensively and sometimes exclusively from the self-understandings of activist leaders, sometimes overcomes the inclination to think *critically* about such effort. Nonetheless the project of publicizing civic renewal initiatives is also of great value, and civil society advocates working in this vein have made it clear that while Progressive politics at the level of the national state may be stalled, when one examines the landscape of American society more carefully one will discover a vigorous civil society politics. As Harry Boyte and Nancy Kari put it in *Building America: The Democratic Promise of Public Work*, one of the key texts of the civic renewal genre: "For all our problems and fears as a nation, civic energy abounds. Americans are not uncaring or apathetic about public affairs. In fact, a rich array of civic work in many diverse settings is evident across the country."[14] Partly in response to the practical limitations of Progressive social policy, partly in response to the ideological disrepute of ambitious Progressive policy visions, and partly as a result of very pragmatic considerations, citizens and civic groups have developed important, innovative practices worth taking very seriously as forms of democratic practice for a post-progressive age. Some examples:

* Many neoprogressives note that the dramatic decline of the American labor movement has had harmful distributional and civic consequences, eroding the principal means of working-class civic engagement and social capital, and thereby exacerbating economic inequality.[15] A hallmark of many neoprogressive proposals is thus a substantial revision of Federal labor law to facilitate union organizing and certification elections and to eliminate long-standing Taft-Hartley restrictions on secondary boycotts, thereby strengthening the organized labor movement that was at the heart of Progressive reform in the twentieth century. But such proposals are politically stalled, lacking any significant chance of being taken seriously by the Democratic party; and the labor movement is stuck at approximately 10 percent of the workforce organized. While the AFL-CIO under the leadership of John Sweeney may have halted a long-term membership decline, and while it may have demonstrated some success in its electoral activities on behalf of Democratic candidates, it has done little to reverse the dramatic weakening of labor's broad political influence over the past two decades.[16] Yet in the face of this political weakness, labor activists, working in conjunction with the AFL-CIO and with forward-looking union leaders, have pioneered a range of innovative efforts, such as cross-border solidarity networks; campaigns against child labor and sweatshop labor; student efforts to support "living

wage" arrangements on university campuses; and Jobs With Justice efforts to support "living wage" ordinances and community tribunals to hear worker grievances and to publicize employer maltreatment of workers. Such efforts, most notably the living wage movement, sometimes seek to influence public policy, typically at the local rather than the national level.[17] Sometimes, as in the widely publicized demonstrations against the World Trade Organization in Seattle, Washington, D.C., and Los Angeles, they seek to protest national public policy. But more often they seek to mobilize civic resources, to press specific grievances, and to influence public opinion, shifting public discourse and building solidarity for workers without substantially altering the balance of power between classes or effecting a dramatic change in public policy.[18]

In *Reclaiming America: Nike, Clean Air, and the New National Activism*, for example, Randy Shaw documents the way in which human rights, labor, and religious activists joined together to pressure Nike to reform its overseas labor practices, which sanctioned repressive and abusive labor relations and extremely low wages in Third World countries, and indirectly generated a worldwide race to the bottom regarding wages and working conditions for garment workers.[19] This campaign involved unions, most notably UNITE (the Needletrades union). But it also involved a variety of other religious and civic groups, from the Interfaith Center on Corporate Responsibility to the Campaign for Labor Rights and Global Exchange. The campaign's outcome was neither a collective bargaining agreement nor a piece of national legislation, but simply a "voluntary accord" between Nike and its critics, brokered by the Clinton administration, that required Nike voluntarily to limits its overseas abuses; to pay so-called prevailing wages; and to submit to voluntary forms of quasi-independent monitoring of its labor practices. This accord also led to the formation of a corporatist organization, the Apparel Industry Partnership (AIP), intended to encourage other apparel manufacturers to undertake similar measures. Subsequent to these developments, the AIP spawned another organization, the Fair Labor Association (FLA), designed to bring together corporations, labor rights groups, and universities behind a program to limit sweatshop abuses. And, in response to the corporate biases of the FLA, student activists associated with United Students Against Sweatshops, working in tandem with the AFL-CIO, UNITE, and other worker organizations, formed the Workers' Right Consortium (WRC) as an alternative to the corporatist FLA that pursues strategies of independent corporate monitoring, and have pressed almost one hundred American universities to affiliate with it.

Significant momentum against sweatshop labor has thus been generated by these numerous campaigns. In many ways, the effects of such activity have been quite limited, and it is clear that such campaigns cannot bring the force of law to bear against corporate abuse. As critics point out, "prevailing wages" in most Third World countries are abominably low, and labor law in these countries affords few rights to workers. Voluntary accords such as the one brokered with Nike, and such as the ones being pursued by both the FLA and the WRC—which in different ways both seek to promote corporate responsibility through forms of collaboration between unions, labor activists, universities, and corporations—do very little to alter such harsh realities. They similarly do little in broad terms to affect global wage rates or to put an end to the tendency of global sweatshop conditions to depress the wages of American workers. Nonetheless they can effect some measure of change in those particular factories that become the focus of public attention, and through this perhaps create small ripple effects of change. Beyond this, they help to raise public awareness about labor issues and to express solidarity with poorly treated workers here and abroad.[20] As Shaw concedes, the anti-Nike campaign has produced "an almost revolutionary shift in America's consciousness about Nike, the garment industry, and the global economy since 1992."[21] Such efforts are not the result of mass movement activity; they do not substantially enhance the bargaining or political power of organized labor, either in Third World countries or in the United States; and they do not add up to a large-scale public policy agenda. Nonetheless they do have some important if limited effects upon economic life and upon the process of political empowerment itself. This is why activists such as Shaw have seized upon them.[22]

- In the face of declining political support and federal funding for vigorous environmental regulation, new civil society approaches have emerged to supplement and sometimes replace top-down bureaucratic regulation of corporations: new forms of deliberation and negotiation about hazardous waste disposal and appropriate risk that include business, local government, environmental activists, and civic associations; public information campaigns about toxic substances, such as the Right to Know Network and Citizens's Clearinghouse on Toxic Waste; civic monitoring of pollution and waste disposal; local green space ordinances, community land trusts, and environmental stewardship; and good neighbor agreements. What has come to be called the "civic environmentalism" model comprises a repertoire of innovative forms of partnership and stakeholding designed to allow local, place-based communities to develop modes of consensus, or at least levels of mutual understanding and trust, about questions of acceptable risk, the costs and benefits of different kinds of toxic cleanups, tradeoffs between jobs and the environment, and the most appropriate methods of managing forests, watersheds, and other environmentally sensitive areas.[23] These techniques are partly a response to declining federal ability and inclination to impose environmental solutions.[24] But they are also the result of a learning process that has taught many environmental activists that there are no cost-free ways to make environmental decisions and that bureaucratic regulation is often inferior to consensus-building and civic responsibility. In their book *Civic Innovation in America,* Sirianni and Friedland present an impressive inventory of such efforts, which have sprung up across the country, and have worked, in fairly mundane and unpublicized ways, to collaboratively resolve environmental problems at the local level. Here too, the results of such innovations are varied, and, unsurprisingly given their modus operandi, such results tend to be localized. But, as Sirianni and Friedland document, they are not without effect upon environmental policy and upon local politics.[25] Indeed, civic environmentalism has moved beyond collaborative approaches to the environment to address broader issues related to urban sprawl, "local self-reliance," and "sustainable development." Communities across the United States have thus taken up the theme of civic responsibility to support new modes of land-use regulation and regional planning that promote urban density and "compact urban form," neighborhood preservation, environmentally sustainable agriculture, and locally owned business.[26]

• In the absence of a massive and ambitious federal effort to revitalize impoverished inner cities through public housing subsidy and construction, job creation, and the serious enhancement of public education, a range of less ambitious and in many ways ad hoc efforts to address urban problems have sprung up throughout the United States: local nonprofit social service agencies that offer child care, support for the victims of domestic abuse, temporary shelter, and job-training; Community Development Corporations that seek to leverage public, private, and philanthropic funds to revitalize neighborhoods through the construction of low-cost housing, the establishment of neighborhood-based health clinics and cooperatives, and the promotion of neighborhood-based retail outlets, banks, shopping centers, and other businesses; community development banks that bridge major financial institutions and inner-city communities, countering the effects of redlining and making funds available for community development; community organizations facilitated by the Industrial Areas Foundation, such as East Brooklyn Congregations, which pioneered the Nehemiah Project of building low-cost housing, and Communities Organized for Public Service, which has organized in support of a range of redevelopment efforts in San Antonio; and innovative, locally oriented third-sector programs designed to build human and social capital, such as YouthBuild, which trains inner-city youth to renovate and construct low-cost housing and at the same time develops general job skills, and the Algebra Project, which seeks to combine innovative curricular methods with community organizing to enhance mathematical literacy among at-risk, inner-city youth.[27] According to one of the most articulate advocates of such civil society efforts, they have generated "a surprising legacy of hope as Americans of good spirit have stepped in to do a job that needed to be done . . . we can look to these small-scale, local efforts to find responses to the problems of poverty that are not only more effective but more humane than our current social service and welfare programs."[28]

WHY CIVIL SOCIETY INITIATIVES DO NOT OFFER AN ALTERNATIVE TO PROGRESSIVISM

Civil society efforts such as the ones noted above clearly hold substantial promise as examples of the way ordinary citizens and grassroots civic organizations can effect a measure of change through their own means. While it is easy to miss the forest for the trees, and to ignore what is actually going on civically on the ground, in particular communities, typically in unobtrusive and unpublicized ways, it is important not to lose sight of these efforts. For politics is difficult work. In the words of Max Weber, it is a "slow boring of hard boards." Our sensationalist and media-saturated culture obscures this in its reduction of politics to celebrity gossip, electoral horseraces, and professional punditry. For this reason civil society efforts are important for their practical value but also for their *exemplary* value, as instances of "civic virtue" and dedicated "public work" that might and should be emulated and extended.

Nonetheless, there are also dangers to exaggerating the significance of these efforts. For such efforts are typically patently inadequate to the problems they address. New labor networks and antisweat campaigns may furnish valuable support and solidarity to workers struggling against the ill effects of untrammeled free trade and financial globalization. They may produce public scrutiny of corporate labor practices and pressure corporate leaders to amend egregious abuses. But such networks have little effect on the ability of workers in the United States or elsewhere to collectively bargain about wages but also about working conditions, job security, and the long-term effects of investment decisions. And they have just as little effect on the possibilities of national policies regarding employment, trade, or long-term, sustainable development. Such efforts are thus no substitute for a coherent political agenda or an activist public policy centered on the concerns of workers and their families.[29]

Similarly, civic environmentalism can help citizens to negotiate the terms by which environmental degradation is abated or remedied, and to collaborate in local deliberative processes about managed growth and environmental sustainability. But such efforts by themselves can do little to affect broader environmental policies regarding acid rain, or global warming, or even regarding the cessation of simple environmental point-pollution. Here there can be no substitute for a national (and indeed international) regulatory policy capable of articulating uniform standards and supporting well-funded and predictable regulatory enforcement. Yet such a policy requires a mobilization of resources and political will that simply does not currently exist. In such a setting, ongoing practices of production and consumption have a life of their own, and generate a "mobilization of bias" in favor of environmental waste and degradation. The experience of the Chesapeake Bay Foundation is instructive here. The Foundation is presented by Sirianni and Friedland as a model of civic environmentalism. And in many ways it would seem exemplary. It has joined together many local environmental and civic groups, across state boundaries, to call attention to environmental degradation and to promote collaborative stewardship of the Chesapeake Bay. And yet, as the *New York Times* recently reported, this exemplary effort to restore the Chesapeake Bay watershed continues to confront extraordinary obstacles. While in 1987 the group had committed itself to reducing nitrogen pollution by 40 percent, it has succeeded thus far in reducing pollution by only 17 percent. This is because it must contend not simply with the legacy of decades of uncontrolled pollution, but also with an additional 300 *million* pounds of nitrogen pollution every year.[30]

And, of course, the same limits present themselves, in an even more striking way, with regard to the inner cities and to problems of urban poverty and inequality. Even the most elaborate and well-connected civil society efforts come up against broad social trends such as deindustrialization and suburbanization; against massive social problems; and against shortages of funds, bureaucratic delays, and the resistance of bankers, bondholders, corporate elites, and sometimes even municipal unions and social service agencies.[31] To offer just one example, the story of Sandtown, an inner-city neighborhood of Baltimore, is often cited as a civic renewal success story. And with good reason. For an impressive partnership of city government, community organizations, and philanthropists has supported a number of innovative housing, job training, youth development, and educational initiatives. And yet, as Peter Edelman—who has extolled this effort as a model—points out, these successes are limited and have come hard. It is worth quoting him at length: "Sandtown is still a poor neighborhood. Many of its adult residents are at a point where positive change is hard for them. There are still too many influences, both at home and on the street, that pull children in the wrong direction. Drug use seems to have actually increased. Nonmarital births are still four times the national rate. Two of the elementary schools have improved phenomenally, but it is not yet even near the truth to say that the school system is consistently turning out job-ready graduates from Sandtown. . . . The job situation is little better."[32] This, keep in mind, is a civic renewal *success* story. But Edelman's comments make clear how difficult success really is, even in those rare settings where "success" can plausibly be claimed at all.

In each of these domains, it would seem, we are presented with broad and systemic public problems whose solution would require equally broad and systemic public policy. And yet what civil society offers tends to be ad hoc, localized, voluntarist, and often voluntary. What civil society offers is short on money and short on what political scientists call "the authoritative allocation of values." These are precisely what Progressivism offered at the turn of the last century, and what Progressive public policy in its subsequent iterations during the New Deal and Great Society periods has always offered: a clear, coherent, national policy agenda for attacking social problems, for bringing them, as it were, to heel, and for substituting an overarching public purposiveness and public power for the anarchy of the market and the automatism of society. To be sure, civil society efforts are genuine *efforts*, and as such they are not without effect. They mobilize a certain kind of civic power that is constituted by the concerted energies of diverse citizens working together. They tap practical idealism, they generate civic confidence, and they promote problem-solving experiences that are distinctive and worthy.[33] Such efforts, in other words, make a difference. But they do not typically mobilize *political power*. They do not generate organizational forms or ideological commitments that might render them capable of offsetting the power of privileged elites and of supporting a substantial political or policy agenda. To the extent that this is true, civil society efforts do not and cannot represent a solution to the problems that neoprogressives seek to address.[34]

Of course, few proponents of civil society would contend that voluntary efforts by themselves could succeed in solving pressing social problems. Even such conservative civil society advocates as Robert Woodson of the National Center for Neighborhood Enterprise recognize that governmental support for civil society efforts is indispensable to their success.[35] In every domain in which civil society initiatives have been lauded, it is fairly clear that these initiatives have thrived not as alternatives to public policy but as the beneficiaries of a supportive public policy. What Sirianni and Friedland observe about civic environmentalism is true in general: "it serves as a complement to, not a substitute for, regulation. A strong federal role is often required to trigger civic approaches."[36] But civil society advocates often fail to take the full measure of the significance of this reliance of civil society efforts on public policy at a time of liberal political weakness. Sirianni and Friedland's *Civic Innovation in America* offers a case study of this failure to attend to the significance of liberal political debilitation, a failing that is all the more instructive because their book is the most empirically sound, careful, and discriminating account of such efforts to have emerged in the past decade.

Sirianni and Friedland catalogue a range of efforts that have emerged in four domains—community development, environmentalism, health policy, and public journalism. In each case they carefully detail the strengths, weaknesses, and dynamics of the efforts under consideration. But they do more than describe a range of "civic innovations." They insist that these innovations are linked together in what they call a "broader civic renewal movement . . . with common language, shared practices, and networked relationships across a variety of arenas."[37] That these innovations share common themes—the importance of active citizenship, the danger of bureaucratism, the importance of pragmatic collaboration— seems clear, just as it seems clear that they are commonly promoted by a core network of philanthropies that includes the National Civic League, the Kettering Foundation, and the Pew Charitable Trusts. But the broader significance of these efforts is less clear. Sirianni and Friedland seem genuinely ambivalent here. On the one hand their text is infused with an explicit "hopefulness" and by a sense that these civic innovations are transforming American public life. "Over the past decades," they write, "[Americans] have created forms of civic practice that that are far more sophisticated in grappling with complex public problems and collaborating with highly diversified social actors than have ever existed in American history." Amidst the worrisome signs of civic disaffection documented by Robert Putnam and others, they maintain, "there is already clear evidence of the kinds of civic innovation that could anchor and instruct broad revitalization strategies in the coming years."[38] The broad democratic promise of these efforts is the major theme of their text.

On the other hand, they note the serious difficulties confronting such a revitalization. "We are deeply aware," they write, "of the many obstacles that exist and the great uncertainty—even profound disagreement— about what a vital civic democracy might mean at the beginning of the twenty-first century. The story we tell is thus not only one of innovation and learning, but also one of roadblocks and detours, struggles and failures. Some of the failures, to be sure, have provided occasion for further learning, but others demonstrate the difficulty of bringing innovations to scale, embedding them in policy design, and creating a politics that will sustain them."[39] When writing in this vein they present the broader project of democratic revitalization as a profoundly difficult task. They thus observe that "without a powerful movement capable of shifting the tides, too much of the vital public work and innovation of citizens analyzed in our core chapters will remain invisible and segmented, unable to inspire broad and vigorous commitment, and unable to redefine the underlying dynamics of 'politics as usual.'"[40] Here the "movement for civic renewal" becomes something of a moral *imperative* rather than an existing state of affairs, and their argument a call to arms rather than a descriptive account. For it may be that without such a movement meaningful change will be impossible.[41] But this does not mean that such a movement is likely to be forthcoming. Like Harry Boyte's earlier *Backyard Revolution*, which, as they acknowledge, first made the case over two decades ago for the importance of such civil society efforts, *Civic Innovation in America* is not simply an analysis but itself a brief for a particular vision of civic renewal, whereby a broad convergence of interest is anticipated and endorsed.[42] Sirianni and Friedland are to be admired for the way they link description and prescription. And their hopefulness cannot simply be dismissed. For, as they pragmatically concede in their more critical moments, the innovations they admire *could* anchor "broad revitalization strategies." But these innovations also might *not* have this effect. Indeed, while their analysis demonstrates beyond doubt the affinities shared by the many efforts they describe, that these efforts together even comprise a "movement" is far from clear.

For a political movement typically involves more than certain common symbolic frames and some degree of overlapping memberships. It also involves a common substantive vision and a sense of historical destiny and forward *movement* toward the achievement of this vision. A political movement, arguably, requires a *teleology*, a grand narrative within which particular efforts acquire larger meaning.[43] It is not clear that the civic efforts they discuss share any such teleology. Sirianni and Friedland admit as much, explicitly underscoring what sets the "civic renewal movement" apart from other social movements of the past and constitutes its genuine distinctiveness. It is worth quoting them at length:

Because the civic renewal movement is not primarily a rights or justice movement, it cannot rely on the metaphors, frames, strategies, or tactical repertoires of recent democratic movements. It cannot inspire action on the basis of unconditional claims to rights or righteous struggles against clearly defined oppressors. It cannot invoke metaphors of unambiguous good or evil or moral resistance in the face of power. It cannot capture and focus public attention through mass protests, marches on Washington, boycotts, strikes, freedom rides, and sit-ins, nor can it count on repression by authorities to galvanize widespread support. It cannot expect dramatic court decisions to energize activists or to secure significant new levers of power and representation.... And while legislation could certainly enact 'policy designs for democracy' that help build civic capacity in specific areas, a civic renewal movement cutting across many institutional sectors cannot hope to build its networks through advocacy coalitions and lobbying for specific laws.[44]

This is an extraordinary paragraph, for it suggests that while civil society efforts surely comprise *something* worth discussing, admiring, and indeed emulating, they do not necessarily comprise a movement at all, but rather a heterogeneous, pluralistic, fractious assemblage of particular and local activities and aspirations with little political unity or historical directionality whatsoever. This sense is further reinforced by Sirianni and Friedland's concluding argument—that the "movement" is and ought to remain beyond partisan political competition. While they clearly lean toward the Democratic party, believing it the most suitable partisan vehicle of civic initiative, they insist that what is most distinctive and vital about civic renewal is its communitarian, collaborative, and pragmatic ethos. Such civil society efforts, they insist, draw their energy from a sense of civic responsibility that is in important respects *antipolitical*. Direct linkage to conventional political organizations and movements, they hold, "has little relevance to the work of civic renewal that needs to occur in all kinds of institutional and professional settings, from schools, universities, and hospitals to corporations, social service nonprofits, and public agencies. Meeting the major challenges in these settings . . . has little to gain from politicization and much to lose." For, according to Sirianni and Friedland, direct politicization encourages adversarial rather than collaborative orientations; it encourages "rights talk" and other insistent discourses about justice and injustice and the political remediation of wrong; and it focuses too much of its energy on the satisfaction of "interests that can be served by state regulatory, social welfare, and redistributive policies."[45] Politicization, in other words, implicates a Progressive liberal project that Sirianni and Friedland consider outmoded and indeed counterproductive because it requires the empowerment of bureaucratic state institutions but also because it is likely to generate powerful political opposition.

In making this argument Sirianni and Friedland's book merges into the broader discourse of "the third way" that has risen to prominence in the past decade, largely in connection with the electoral victories, and policy agendas, of Bill Clinton and Tony Blair. The "third way" is a slogan that has been deployed, with substantial effect, by American New Democrat and British New Labour politicians seeking political power in societies that had experienced the electoral defeat of progressive or social democratic parties and the political ascendancy of Reaganite and Thatcherite conservatism. Sidney Blumenthal, erstwhile Clintonite, has described the third way as "the practical experience of two leading politicians [Clinton and Blair] who win elections, operate in the real world, and understand the need, in a global economy, to find common solutions for common problems." Beneath the slogan, the third way connotes both a political strategy and a policy agenda. The political strategy is to move, in the words of Anthony Giddens, "beyond left and right," and to seek a broad consensus in the center of the political spectrum, at what is called, interchangeably, the "radical center," the "vital center," and the "active middle."[46] The basic point of this strategy is to acknowledge that neither Progressive liberalism nor social democratic reformism can any longer rely on the support of an organized and powerful working class, and both must instead make their accommodation with the forces of deindustrialization and suburbanization and the hegemony of market values that have weakened working-class solidarities.[47] Accompanying this strategy is a policy agenda associated with the retrenchment of the welfare state and the politics of national regulation, and an effort to "actively promote" the opportunities associated with private markets, third-wave technologies, and third-sector, philanthropic activity. In the name of "flexibility," third-wave politics endorses a dramatic scaling back of the role of the national state and a virtual repudiation of the Progressive legacy in the name of "progress" itself.

In the United States, this "third way" has been associated with the Democratic Leadership Council and the Progressive Policy Institute under the leadership of Al Fromm and Will Marshall. Marshall nicely summarized this third-wave approach in an essay, "A New Fighting Faith," published in the DLC's *New Democrat* in the fall of 1996 in support of the Clinton reelection campaign. It is worth quoting Marshall at length:

> The party's old faith, New Deal progressivism, has run its historic course. In his January State of the Union address, President Clinton made it official when he declared that "the era of big government is over." The venerable New Deal creed was undone both by its great success in creating a large middle class that now sees itself more burdened than benefited from government, and by its undue reliance on outdated bureaucracies and top-down programs to meet the needs of a fast changing society. . . . For today's progressives, there is no challenge more compelling than the need to replace a governance model developed for the Industrial Age—an era characterized by large, centralized institutions. . . . The new paradigm for progressive government springs from a simple insight: since we can no longer reply on big institutions to take care of us, we must create policies and institutions that enable us to take care of ourselves.[48]

Marshall's so-called new progressivism thus repudiates a strong state and a vigorous public policy in the name of "equal opportunity," "mutual responsibility," and "self-governing citizenship." In the place of a supposedly heavy-handed and sclerotic state, the New Democrats exalt voluntarism, in economics and in ethics, in trade policy, social regulation, and social service delivery. For Marshall this "new progressivism" is a partisan strategy suited to Democratic electoral victories.[49] But the affinities between this approach and the "new citizenship" endorsed by "compassionate conservatives" such as Michael Joyce, Michael Woodson, and William Schambra, who are closely associated with the political agenda of the Republican party under the leadership of George W. Bush, should be obvious. These compassionate conservatives tend to be *civic* Republicans who sound the same themes—fiscal austerity, social solidarity, and civic engagement—as their New Democratic counterparts.[50] The "new citizenship" is, ideologically speaking, a *bipartisan* approach well adapted to a political terrain characterized by liberal exhaustion and substantial conservative success in delegitimizing a Progressive agenda.[51]

My point is not that Sirianni and Friedland are proponents of the "third way" or of the rightward shift of the Democratic party engineered by the Democratic Leadership Council and solidified under the eight-year reign of Clinton-Gore. For they do not so much as even mention the third way idea. They are genuinely concerned with civil society as a site of practical problem-solving and civic engagement, and not with the world of partisan politics. They are interested primarily in what is most innovative and hopeful about civil society initiatives and not with the broader historical and political context within which these initiatives operate. Unlike most of the arguments put forth by both neoprogressives and "third way" advocates, Sirianni and Friedland's analysis is adamantly antipolitical in the conventional sense. Electoral strategy and partisan maneuvering simply do not interest them. But there is nevertheless a strong affinity between their gloss on the "civic renewal movement" and the anti-Progressive rhetoric of the third way.

Indeed, the point of strongest intersection is one they do mention—the Reinventing Citizenship Project organized in 1993 by William Galston, a communitarian political theorist, long-time Democratic issues adviser, and White House Deputy Assistant for Domestic Policy in Clinton's first term. Under Galston's leadership this project brought together many of the academic and civic leaders of the "civic renewal movement." It organized meetings, conducted public hearings, published reports, and drafted policy proposals and public declarations on the themes of civic renewal and reinventing citizenship. Sirianni and Friedland—active participants in this process—describe this effort with a measure of legitimate enthusiasm. The enthusiasm seems legitimate because the project involved many interesting people and ideas and seemed to signify a real openness to civic innovation at the highest levels of government. But they offer only a single sentence by way of an account of the ultimate political fate of these noble efforts: "The administration, however, proved unable to focus on this and other related initiatives once the congressional elections of 1994 took center stage."[52] They do note that the White House continued to consult with academics linked to the civic renewal discourse, and that it even "fashioned active citizenship themes" for use in the 1995 State of the Union Address and the 1996 presidential campaign. But what they do not do is offer any account of White House follow-through, or of any serious, programmatic or policy outcome associated with the Reinventing Citizenship Project. The reason they fail to discuss this is because there does not appear to have *been* any such outcome. For the Clinton administration "reinventing citizenship" appears to have been a "theme" rather than a political vision.[53] As a rhetoric, new citizenship themes have clearly well served a Democratic party leadership intent on unburdening liberalism of its Progressive liberal past, on dismantling the welfare state and promoting global free trade, and on emphasizing the assumption of civic duties at a time in which there seems to be little political interest in enforcing social or economic rights. For the new citizenship discourse in many ways validates the political retrenchment of New Democrat liberalism, reaffirming its insistence that a regulatory state is necessarily corrupt and disempowering, and that true civic responsibility requires a substantial repudiation of such a state in the name of voluntarism.

At the same time, it is important to note that if "the new citizenship" was for the Clinton administration primarily a "theme" and a rhetoric, its distinctive features *as* a rhetoric at least deserve note. In a political context in which social Darwinist themes have played an important role in delegitimizing liberalism, and in which forms of ethnic and religious fundamentalism have come to prevail throughout many parts of the world, the discourse of "new citizenship" and civic responsibility emphatically articulates liberal and universalist values. The appeal to "civility" is no grand answer to the problems confronting American society. But it is to be preferred to rhetorics of incivility that demonize or vilify particular groups and essentialize individual competition and social conflict. At the same time, when this appeal is unaccompanied by a serious and coherent policy agenda at a time of intensified social and economic insecurity, it can easily assume a moralizing tone that smacks of hypocrisy. New citizenship discourse too often has suffered from this (though, as I suggest below, it need not necessarily suffer from it).[54]

To point this out is not to present the "third way" as a politics of betrayal. To the contrary, the third way represents a savvy political strategy of coming to terms with changed social, economic, demographic,

and political conditions. Those who charge New Democrats with betrayal, however sincere and well-intentioned they may be, simply fail to
reckon with these changing conditions. As Lars-Erik Nelson has pointed
out, Bill Clinton, after all—the only truly successful Democratic presidential politician since the mid-1960s—was never a left or Progressive
Democrat. He was a moderate governor of a Southern state who was
elected to office in 1992 with 43 percent of the popular vote—hardly a
mandate for progressive change; who had already demonstrated his
commitment to the DLC strategy of "modernizing" the Democratic
party by shifting it to the right; who was supported by the smallest congressional majority of any president elected in the twentieth century;
and who confronted a Republican party that had moved far to the right
and that had successfully shifted political discourse to the right. In Nelson's words, "there was a great political middle to be grabbed, and Clinton grabbed it."[55]

Clinton may well have betrayed his own idealistic rhetorical flourishes.
And he surely treated both the rhetoric of liberalism and the rhetoric of
civic responsibility in an opportunistic fashion that, alas, demoralized
many, avid compatriots and lukewarm supporters alike, who took seriously his rhetoric of renewal. Further, he surely made tactical mistakes—
most notably regarding health care reform—that may have limited his
subsequent ability to live up to even a small portion of the promise that
many originally attached to his presidency. But, given the balance of political forces that were arrayed behind him and against him, it is hard to
imagine him performing much differently than he did.[56] Like most politicians, he took the path of least resistance to electoral success. If that path
was essentially a neoliberal one, this can hardly be blamed on Clinton.
For, truth be told, there existed little backing for anything more Progressive and many obstacles in the way of a more ambitious agenda. Clinton
is not without blame for many of his failings. But neither is Clinton the
demiurgic betrayer of liberalism that many of his critics on the left believe
him to be. He was, simply, a creature of his times, a Democratic leader at
a time when the sources of liberal vigor had dried up and the Democratic
party had become, well, for all intents and purposes, Republican. Clinton
surely aided and abetted this transsubstantiation. But he was hardly its
prime mover.[57]

Similarly, to note the affinities between the discourse of "civic renewal"
and the third way policies of the New Democratic Clinton administration
is to impugn neither the motives nor the achievements of the proponents
of "civic renewal" and the civil society initiatives they endorse. As I have
argued in this book, I agree with Sirianni and Friedland, and indeed with
Will Marshall and other proponents of "third way" thinking, that Progressive liberalism is largely anachronistic, the product of economic and

political conditions that no longer obtain. I also agree that meaningful partisan political contention in American national politics is likely to take place in the "active middle," on the terrain of a rough political consensus on the impracticality and undesirability of ambitious social democratic regulation, the virtues of economic globalization and the market, and the centrality of a "civic" politics centered on social solidarity and voluntarism rather than on vigorous politicized demands for socioeconomic justice.[58]

In such a political environment Sirianni and Friedland are right. Collaborative approaches often have the greatest chance of practical success. For those interested in crafting such approaches partisan entanglement often promises little reward for civil society initiatives—for political vision or substantial funding seem forthcoming from neither party—and many costs. At the same time, once one proceeds from the premise that the policy debate is severely constricted, it is both possible and advisable to work, pragmatically, with all those, conservative and liberal, religious and secular, business-oriented and labor-oriented, who are committed to practical solutions to public problems. In the domains of neighborhood and community organizing, civic environmentalism, the experimental practice of deliberative democracy in local settings, philanthropic activity—especially United Way fundraising, which is a major source of social service funding in most American local communities—and even faith-based initiatives in social service delivery, there exist collaborative opportunities to work effectively across partisan and ideological boundaries.[59] Such work may not be where the partisan political "action" is. And it is a far cry from more ambitious visions of policy innovation and political transformation. But it is most assuredly where much of the civic energy and action really *is* in American society today, and it would be sheer foolishness to deny this.

My problem is not with the civil society focus of the partisans of "civic renewal," nor with the disposition of these partisans to discern promise in such collaborative efforts, and to promote hopefulness about their meaning. My problem is with the celebratory and credulous tone with which much of this tends to be discussed by civic renewal writers. For while these writers display great knowledgeability about the rhetorics and tactics of civic renewal, and while their accounts typically contain much insight and perceptiveness regarding how such efforts work on the ground, they tend to be too buoyant in their view of what such efforts can and do in fact accomplish. On some level, I think, this is due to the hermeneutical and interpretive approaches that these writers choose to adopt. Committed to the agency of ordinary citizens and to the importance of civic self-understandings and purposes, these writers typically employ a narrative method. They assume the role of civic storytellers, whose task it is to tell inspiring stores of civic innovation that might extend and deepen future innovation. This is an admirable task. The closer one gets to the ground of activism, the more one may feel compelled, and perhaps even called, to this task of civic self-promotion. The consequence of such a vocation, however, is the substitution of an interest in meaning for an interest in *causality and consequence*. What is lacking in too much of the civic renewal literature is a serious reckoning with the causal *constraints* under which civil society efforts operate. These constraints, which severely limit the aspirations of neoprogressives to revive a Progressive policy agenda, limit the aspirations of civic renewal as well.

THE SISYPHEAN TASK OF CIVIL SOCIETY POLITICS

Civil society efforts thus both do and do not offer an alternative to Progressivism. They are promising examples of civic initiative and pragmatic problem solving. They may well be the only game in town. But they are limited, and frustrating, in ways that civic renewal advocates rarely admit. The problem with the discourse of civil society is not its post-progressivism but its *credulity*, its failure to see the *tragedy* in the decline of Progressive liberalism. Civic renewal writers, of the left and the right—and, admittedly, for the partisans of civic renewal these lines are increasingly blurred—properly discern the poverty of Progressivism and properly seek to discern the redeeming promise in Progressivism's decline. They rightly appreciate the innovative character of contemporary civil society efforts and understand that these efforts are the products of genuine learning experiences among activists and elites in the post-1960s period. But they present as an unambiguous gain what is in fact a deeply ambiguous and problematic achievement. They insufficiently theorize the fact that these efforts are largely the product of learning *under severe duress*, and that this duress is due to the political weakening of "progressive" forces, which has liberated social and economic processes for good but also *for ill*, creating new "opportunities" and "flexibilities" but also new *vulnerabilities* and anxieties.

While the welfare state surely had its share of pathologies, the decline of the Progressive agenda and of the regulatory state has simply unleashed the equally potent pathologies of the "private sphere," including the powerful pathologies of civil society itself. Privatism. Insularity. Greed. Self-absorption. Exclusivism. Ethnic, racial, and sexual resentment. These pathologies cannot simplistically be laid at the feet of a bureaucratic state or the social engineering aspirations of Progressive elites. They are features of contemporary civil society. They by no means exhaust civil society. But neither is civil society a pristine or communitarian site of smooth and edifying social interaction and need satisfaction.[60] The "liberation" of society from social regulation represents a defeat of bureaucracy. But it also represents a serious eclipse of public agencies and public identities. The "new citizenship" this has called forth embodies genuine civic impulses. But its very voluntarism and its partiality serve to vitiate one of the most important features of modern liberal democratic citizenship—its generality and its universality. To this extent, civil society's gain has been civil society's loss as well. The loss is a loss of material resources, but also of the ethical and civic resources associated with a serious commitment to universal citizenship and social justice on the part of the state acting in the name of society as a whole. Civil society discourse typically lacks any appreciation of the *tragedy* of this.

Similarly, while civic renewal may not be strictly a partisan affair, the current partisan *stasis*, resting on a bipartisan political consensus about the desirability of flexible markets and political retrenchment, is hardly supportive of independent civic initiative. For while "third way" liberals and their compassionate conservative compatriots offer rhetorical support for social responsibility and civic engagement, they do not offer a coherent and ambitious program for supporting and funding civil society initiative on a level commensurate with the problems confronting civil society today, Yet at the same time their neoliberal economic commitments help to generate many of the social problems against which ordinary citizens and grass roots civic associations set themselves. In this context, as I have already noted, moral invocations of civility and civic voluntarism and the importance of a sacrificial ethos ring hollow.[61] For civil society needs more than moral earnestness. Civil society needs *help*. A great deal of help. The most honest partisans of civic renewal acknowledge this, as do many of those neoprogressives, such as Theda Skocpol, E. J. Dionne Jr., and Margaret Weir, who have sought critically to engage the partisans of civil society in dialogue about the necessary reliance of civic renewal upon political supports and public policy.[62]

What this means, once again, is that *the political crisis of liberal Progressivism is a problem of enormous proportions for civic renewal*. It is not something that can be ignored on the grounds that civic politics is bipartisan or nonpartisan or "beyond left and right." To be more blunt: the situation that we confront is one where we may well be "beyond left," but *we are not beyond right*. Conservative economic policies have dominated and continue to dominate party-political discourse. American politics today takes place on the terrain of the triumph of market values and institutions.[63] But this is not a natural or ineluctable development or a simple actualization of freedom. It is a *problematic historical outcome*. And civil society is a "solution" that is not commensurate with this problem. Indeed, to the extent that civil society stands alone, it is itself symptomatic of the problem itself rather than its solution. And yet it may be the only viable solution in the sense that no other method of practical response is viable. This, alas, is the tragic bind in which we seem to find ourselves.

I do not believe there is any point in denying this tragic bind or seeking an easy way out of it. An honest reading of the political situation suggests that the prospects for a Progressive revival are dim. This does not mean that a Progressive revival is impossible. Neither does it mean that the effort to craft political coalitions and movements designed to move beyond the current situation and generate a new Progressive hegemony are hopeless. If it would be foolish to credulously anticipate a new Progressive dispensation, it would be no less foolish to adopt a posture of dogmatic incredulity. The truth is that we cannot confidently predict the future. Things may change. Progressive forces may strengthen. A crisis might precipitate the turn toward a more radical agenda—though this may just as likely be a radicalism of the *right* as of the left. The most appropriate approach to such scenarios is simply an experimental openness to new possibilities. But an experimental openness should consist of more than willful optimism or programmatic vision or Rortyean hopefulness. It should draw on a sober historical and social analysis combined with a chastened sense of political realism.

While such a sense of realism would caution against optimism, it would not counsel political despair. For while the national political landscape is bleak, there currently exist some promising examples of seemingly successful efforts to create new Progressively oriented coalitions at the state and local level. In Milwaukee, for example, the Campaign for a Sustainable Milwaukee, a coalition of over one hundred labor and citizen groups, has worked, together with the New Party and liberals within the Democratic party, to achieve substantial influence over the City Council, and to promote regional planning, job training, and living wage initiatives. In Burlington, Vermont, a Progressive Coalition of socialists and liberal Democrats has been able to advance an impressive policy agenda centered around left-liberal values. In Connecticut, the Legislative Electoral Action Program has successfully run citizen-activist candidates for the state legislature, in the process building a base for political and economic reform. In New York, the Working Families Party, a fusion party formed by progressive unions and such activist citizens's organizations as ACORN and Citizen Action, has achieved some modest headway through its cross-endorsements of liberal Democratic candidates. In Los Angeles a progressive coalition of liberals, African Americans, and Hispanics has begun to shift the temper of city politics. In cities across the United States, from Boston to Portland to Baltimore, living wage campaigns linking unions, citizens, and liberal politicians have successfully instituted "living wage ordinances" raising the wage-rates of city-contracted workers and enhancing the local influence of unions.[64]

Each of these efforts exemplifies not simply a civic but a *political* accomplishment, involving the mobilization of party organizations and the winning of electoral offices; and each contains promise. To their partisans each indeed may well represent a harbinger of things to come, and contain the seed of a broad, national Progressive revival. It would be pointless to seek to falsify such hypotheses. But what can be said with some assurance is that to date these efforts have had a limited effect on national politics, at the level of political discourse, party agendas, or public policy. While the jury is not and cannot be out on these efforts, each contains weaknesses as well as strengths. And each confronts profound political obstacles, particularly once they are extended beyond local contexts and treated as models of national renewal. It is true that the original Progressivism itself emerged out of disparate local tumult and experimentation. But it is also true that historical conditions at the turn of the twentieth century supported this emergence, so that in retrospect we can understand how and why such a Progressive coalescence occurred. Unfortunately historical conditions today do not appear similarly supportive. Writing in 1909, Walter Lippmann could plausibly view Progressive reform as the "latent promise" of the present. Such credulity is not, alas, available to us.

AMERICA IN SEARCH OF A PUBLIC PHILOSOPHY?

What then, of politics, in the sense not of partisan struggle but of the practice of public decision making oriented toward a conception of the public good? Is the very idea of "public good" anachronistic? Can or should the pluralistic, fragmented and provisional space of civil society initiative be mobilized on behalf of some overarching sense of public good? Is it necessary for the diverse efforts noted above to add up to something larger, more visionary, or more edifying? Do we need what the political philosopher Michael Sandel has called a new "public philosophy" of citizenship, capable of inspiring citizens to undertake collective projects and of orienting them toward greater, more substantial and inclusive commonalities?

Sandel, for one, is notably ambivalent on this score. On the one hand, he writes in support of a "political agenda informed by civic concerns," and of a "formative project" of engaged, republican citizenship that is intimated, "hinted" and "gestured" at by current civic renewal initiatives.[65] The entire thrust of his book *Democracy's Discontent* is to criticize the inadequacies of contemporary post-1960s liberalism as a materialistic and individualistic "public philosophy," and to suggest the desirability of an alternative, "republican" philosophy of public life. But, on the other hand, he is quite vague about both the substance of such a philosophy and the

collective agents or institutional forms capable of bringing it into existence. While he briefly mentions many of the initiatives discussed above,
he admits that they are "disparate expressions" of citizenship and that
they exist "around the edges of our political discourse and practice." He
thus endorses federalism, less as a constitutional form than as an ideal,
because it "stands for a political vision that offers an alternative to the
sovereign state and the univocal identities that such states require. It suggests that self-government works best when sovereignty is dispersed and
citizenship formed across multiple sites of civic engagement." And he
concludes by asserting that "self-government today . . . requires a politics
that plays out in a multiplicity of settings. . . . [and] requires citizens who
can think and act as multiply situated selves."[66] The clear implication of
these comments is that these civic projects have no substantial focus and
do not converge upon an alternative vision of national much less global
politics.

A similar ambivalence haunts Robert Putnam's *Bowling Alone*. Having
analyzed at great length the current "disappearance of civic America,"
Putnam turns, in his concluding section, to consider "What is To Be
Done?" His account here consists of two arguments. The first argument is
a variation on the neoprogressive theme: just as the Progressive Era was a
moment of civic innovation and vigorous associational activity, he writes,
"we desperately need an era of civic inventiveness to create a renewed set
of institutions and channels for a reinvigorated civic life that will fit the
way we have come to live. Our challenge now is to reinvent the twenty-
first century equivalent of the Boy Scouts or the settlement house of the
United Mine Workers or the NAACP." We need such innovation, Putnam
insists, both to restore civic confidence and because social capital is "not
an alternative to, but a prerequisite for, political mobilization and reform."[67] The second argument is essentially a sermonic call for civic invention and "social capitalism" in six domains. Each of these six calls be-
gins with the invocation "let us find ways to ensure that by 2010" civic
renewal will occur; each reiterates the importance of civic renewal in the
domain in question; and each fails to speak with specificity about how
such renewal might be a meaningful object of public policy, who might
embrace such renewal as a political objective worth fighting for, or how
such renewal might relate to "political mobilization and reform." Putnam,
in short, desires that "social capitalism" should become a unifying political project. He seeks a convergence of interest in renewal on the part of all
of those active in civic life. But he offers no political account of how or why
this convergence might occur.

If my argument is correct, there are good reasons to believe that such a
convergence is not likely to occur. But beyond this, there is something pe-
culiar about the very desire to promote such a convergence. For what is

most distinctive about civil society as a site of civic engagement is precisely its associational plurality, which resists clear political representation. Labor, religious, environmental, community, racial, and other associations form in civil society, and operate there, on a voluntary and particularistic basis, without any necessary or clear overarching political goals. Sometimes such groups form coalitions or work in tandem. Sometimes they work at cross purposes with each other. Civically active women might join together in support of a local soup kitchen or county museum or the Girl Scouts, and yet some may support Planned Parenthood or the National Abortion Rights Action League and others "family values" groups or antiabortion crisis pregnancy centers. Religious congregations and clergy groups might join together to celebrate Martin Luther King Jr. Day and yet disagree strongly on the topic of gay rights. A range of community groups—neighborhood associations, environmental organizations, labor unions, League of Women Voters, Chamber of Commerce, various trade and civic associations—may come together to support organizing forums of "public deliberation" about the economic future of their community, and yet these groups may sharply diverge when it comes to the initiatives and policies they are willing to support. If the site of political innovation today is in the domain of civil society, and if this domain is inherently complex and multivocal, then perhaps it is pointless to hope for some Hegelian synthesis to emerge from it.

Along these lines the record of the Industrial Areas Foundation (IAF) is instructive. The IAF is a fascinating example of civic initiative that is informed by a robust conception of democratic participation and that has been remarkably successful in producing results in a number of major American cities. This combination of idealism and effectiveness is no doubt the reason why so many contemporary writers have invoked the IAF as a model.[68] In his superb recent book *Dry Bones Rattling: Community Building to Revitalize American Democracy*, Mark R. Warren presents the most careful account of the IAF thus far written.[69] Focusing on the successes of IAF organizer Ernesto Cortes Jr., Warren charts the development of an elaborate community organizing network, rooted in the power of San Antonio's Communities Organized for Public Service (COPS), that has extended throughout the state of Texas and indeed has developed a broader presence in the Southwest region as a whole. IAF organizations are broad-based; rooted in local institutions and faith communities; and created on the basis of painstaking face-to-face contact, discussion, and public work. They engage in voluntary community-building initiatives but also practice grassroots political organizing, deploying tactics of nonpartisan political pressure and carefully planned protest to focus public attention on the plight of disadvantaged communities and to demand, and achieve, governmental responses in areas ranging from garbage collection and sewage disposal to affordable housing to public school reform, job training, and employment.

Warren demonstrates that IAF organizing has been effective, in Texas and in other parts of the country, because it is centered in local institutions and is dedicated to grassroots capacity-building. As he writes:

> It is quite easy to dismiss this local organizing in the face of the globalization of the economy. Many analysts jump immediately to an effort to figure out the correct policy, the right issue, to solve local problems. Activists rush to influence the highest levels of power. To do so is a serious mistake. Political and policy elites have much to offer our understanding of public policy, but they can't operate alone. Grand schemes launched by Washington-based advocacy groups often lack the organized backing to be adopted in the political arena. They are not necessarily the most effective policies anyway. Local knowledge, a close understanding of the needs and aspirations of Americans at the ground level, must inform social policy if it is to be effective.[70]

Nonetheless, Warren also recognizes the limits of such organizing. He thus contends that "high-level power is still required" to facilitate such local efforts and to develop public policies commensurate with the problems confronting ordinary American citizens, and notes that "the relentless emphasis on local work . . . has left the IAF ill equipped to undertake national action now that it has the foundation to do so." Like Sandel, and like Putnam, Warren nourishes a lingering hope that the successes of the IAF can be replicated and taken to a higher, national level. He thus concludes by considering what the IAF would need to do to move to this higher level of organizing, and speculating about how the IAF might both facilitate, and serve as a model for, a "national force for political renewal."[71]

Warren is correct to note the limits of IAF strategies and to observe that some kind of national renewal would be necessary in order to more vigorously and comprehensively address the problems of urban America. But the expectation that the IAF might somehow anticipate such a renewal seems to fly in the face of his own analysis of what is so distinctive about the IAF and what accounts for its distinctive success. For the IAF, on his own reading, is premised upon an understanding of power as something created through proximate forms of concerted action (this understanding is indebted to the political philosopher Hannah Arendt). As a matter of strategy and as a matter of principle, the IAF has sought to develop power locally, and to exercise this power in ways that are experimental and issue-specific, and that forswear the establishment of permanent alliances or the identification of permanent adversaries. Such an improvisational modus operandi does not lend itself to national forms of organization, to mass politics, or to ambitious programs of national renewal and redistributive social policy.

What I would suggest is that if the IAF is exemplary, it is exemplary precisely because of its unique and pragmatic combination of civic audacity and *programmatic modesty*. The IAF is perhaps best viewed neither as a promising seed of national renewal nor as a model of civic innovation to be replicated in other places and by other kinds of organizations, but rather as an *example* of effective civic innovation under arduous conditions. Models can be reiterated, replicated, and expanded. Examples can only be emulated. To think of the IAF as an example is to acknowledge that it is not an all-purpose guide to civic initiative and is not the harbinger of something bigger and better than itself. It simply, but crucially, exemplifies some important principles and pragmatic understandings that are worth amplifying, and that might be the basis for a range of efforts across and range of domains. My point is not that the IAF should forswear efforts to organize and to expand its influence in new places. My point is that it would be a mistake to overburden this very impressive civil society innovation with large-scale political expectations that exceed its capacities and that in fact obscure its distinctive modalities and achievements.

What I am suggesting is that the IAF furnishes a useful example of what politics in America today can accomplish. As such, it can be a touchstone for a new political orientation, but in a more modest sense than Sandel, Putnam, and Warren envision, less as an integrative public philosophy or agenda than as an ethos of pragmatic public engagement. Such an ethos would center around the core values of liberal democratic politics. It would promote the value of individual and associational freedom and encourage the exercise of this freedom by conscientious citizens and civic groups. It would foster an appreciation for the pluralism that is endemic to modern social life, and promote civility and the inclination to engage rather than demonize one's adversaries. It would advance the values of civic equality and social solidarity, which entail that a political community is more than a war of each against all, and that questions of inequality of opportunity or advantage are public questions that involve some measure of public responsibility. Most especially, it would promote the idea of democracy itself—the idea that ordinary citizens ought to take responsibility for the problems of their world, and ought to be collaboratively involved in crafting, implementing, and monitoring public solutions to these problems. But it would be distinguished not by the way it philosophically configures these values nor by an integrated vision of public policy believed to actualize these values. It would be distinguished by the understanding that as a matter of politics there is no single "best" way to articulate and to advance these values.

I would submit that instead of anticipating some new integrative vision of public life, we should be attentive to the range of experiments, initiatives, and organizations that currently exist and that are likely to develop and to persist. These are not likely to be informed by a common vision and they are not likely to converge upon a common vision. They are likely to function in a hostile political environment in which social and economic "progress" is the source of advantage but also difficulty, disappointment, and risk, and in which national political organizations and state institutions are incapable of generating either the public vision or the political will capable of bringing such problems to heel.

To propose this is not to dismiss or disparage more hopeful scenarios and projects. It is not my intention to limit political vision to the local and fragmentary. While the kind of skeptical analysis I have provided runs the risk of cynicism, this is a risk that I have tried to avoid. Hopefulness and visionary thinking and ambitious policy agendas have their place in politics. Without them, democratic politics could never rise above the prosaic and the banal. Without them, democratic politics could never have even begun to institute social justice and progressive social policy. But hopefulness, and vision, also have the potential to limit political thinking, by furnishing a measure of optimism and comfort where it is not warranted, and by encouraging a kind of overreaching that can be dispiriting and self-defeating. The comfort of neoprogressivism is the belief that historical forces are tending in a Progressive direction and that a sufficient grasp of these forces can unlock the strategic key to Progressive triumph. The comfort of those partisans of civil society who have reconciled themselves to the impoverishment of Progressivism is that the prose of everyday civic life is sufficient to sustain public problem solving and civic renewal. In my view both forms of credulity are mistaken. History does not bode well for progressivism. But neither is a robust civil society sufficient to redeem what Herbert Croly called the promise of American life. The irony is that at this moment of American celebration, this promise may be in crucial respects beyond redemption.

The asymmetry between the problems we confront and the likely means of their solution should not be a cause for despair. For there continue to exist democratic energies and vehicles for their partial realization. These warrant critical support. Their example ought to be promoted. The values they embody ought to be elucidated, and publicized, and made the topic of civic self-reflection and civic education. This is the truth of the proponents of civic renewal. But these energies, and their vehicles, are unlikely to generate large-scale, progressive social reform. The Progressive vision of social intelligence and social policy has produced much that is good, but it is simply too ambitious, and too bereft of political supports, to be realized under current conditions. Local elections can be won by "progressives." Local initiatives and political experiments can have an accumulating impact on public awareness and public policy. But the project of marshalling a new hegemony is anachronistic, and not likely to succeed.

More localized civil society initiatives are surely insufficient to this task. They cannot help us to master our difficulties. Citizens who engage in them can experience a sense of efficacy and perhaps some measure of practical satisfaction. But they are also bound to experience such efforts as limited, partial, and frustrating. Learning to live with these frustrations, and persist without resentment in spite of them, may prove to be the most important civic virtue of our time.

In Albert Camus's novel *The Plague*, Dr. Rieux, the heroic leader of the resistance, is asked what gives him the confidence to persist in his struggle against an injustice that seems virtually implacable. "I've no more," he responds, "than the pride that's needed to keep me going. I have no idea what's awaiting me, or what will happen when all this ends. For the moment I know this: there are sick people and they need curing." The world, he avers, is bounded by death; and our victories on behalf of life are always temporary, always fragile. "Yet this is not reason," he concludes, "for giving up the struggle." Camus's Rieux is a slightly more heroic version of Sisyphus, who, on Camus's telling, also confronts a tragic fate. Sisyphus is doomed to persist without end in the impossible task of raising his stone to the top of the mountain. His fate is to fail. Such a fate could well cause him to despair. But on Camus's telling he learns that it is not the mountaintop but the rock that is his true fate. His universe henceforth "seems to him neither sterile nor futile. Each atom of that stone, each mineral flake of that night-filled mountain, in itself forms a world. The struggle toward the heights is enough to fill a man's heart. One must imagine Sisyphus happy."[72] Sisyphus's happiness is a tragic happiness. But it is more than despair because Sisyphus is motivated by a value, the value of his own agency, and, so motivated, his struggle, and its always inadequate results, has meaning. Those who interpret the myth of Sisyphus as a story of futility are mistaken. For it is only from the standpoint of the mountaintop that Sisyphus fails.

American democracy faces severe challenges. I do not think that we can in good faith confront the present century with the same optimism, and ambition, with which Progressives confronted the last one. The kinds of democratic responses that are likely to be effective are bound to be partial, limiting, fractious, and in many ways unsatisfying. They are likely to disappoint the modernist quest for mastery and the Progressive faith in the future. And they are likely to frustrate the democratic project of collective self-control and self-governance. Yet it is the great virtue of democracy as a form of politics that it prizes contingency, and experimentation, and critique, and further experimentation, ad infinitum. For in the end politics, even under the most favorable circumstances, is nothing else but the Sisyphean task of constructing provisional solutions to our unmasterable difficulties.

NOTES

1. See Manuel Castells's three-volume *The Information Age: The Rise of the Net-work Society* (London: Blackwell, 1996), *The Power of Identity* (London: Blackwell, 1997), and *End of the Millennium* (London: Blackwell, 1998); Ulrich Beck, *Democracy Without Enemies* (London: Polity, 1998); Anthony Giddens, ed., *The Global Third Way Debate* (London: Polity, 2001); Michael Hardt and Antonio Negri, *Empire* (Cambridge, MA: Harvard University Press, 2001); Paul Hirst and Grahame Thompson, *Globalization in Question* (London: Polity Press, 1999); and Zygmunt Bauman, *Globalization* (London: Polity Press, 1998).

2. Zygmunt Bauman, *Liquid Modernity* (Cambridge, UK: Polity Press, 2000), pp. 1–3, 11.

3. Zygmunt Bauman, *In Search of Politics* (Stanford: Stanford University Press, 1999), pp. 97–98.

4. Robert Putnam, *Bowling Alone: The Collapse and Revival of American Community* (New York: Simon and Schuster, 2000); and Theda Skocpol, "Advocates Without Members: The Recent Transformation of American Civic Life," in Theda Skocpol and Morris P. Fiorina, eds., *Civic Engagement in American Democracy* (Washington, DC: Brookings Institution, 1999), pp. 461–512.

5. Margaret Weir and Marshall Ganz, "Reconnecting People and Politics," in Stanley B. Greenberg and Theda Skocpol, eds., *The New American Majority: Toward a Popular Progressive Politics* (New Haven, CT: Yale University Press, 1997).

6. One of the most perceptive critiques is Harry Boyte's "Off the Playground of Civil Society," *The Good Society*, vol. 9, no. 1 (1999).

7. Jürgen Habermas, "The New Obscurity: The Crisis of the Welfare State and the Exhaustion of Utopian Energies," in *The New Conservatism: Cultural Criticism and the Historians' Debate* (Cambridge, MA: MIT Press, 1989).

8. See Don E. Eberly, *America's Promise: Civil Society and the Renewal of American Culture* (Lanham, MD: Rowman & Littlefield, 1998), and the Council on Civil Society, *A Call to Civil Society: Why Democracy Needs Moral Truths* (New York: Institute for American Values, 1998).

9. See Benjamin R. Barber, *A Place for Us: How to Make Society Civil and Democracy Strong* (New York: Hill and Wang, 1998).

10. See Robert Putnam, *Bowling Alone*, and Richard A. Couto, with Catherine S. Guthrie, *Making Democracy Work Better: Mediating Structures, Social Capital, and the Democratic Prospect* (Chapel Hill: University of North Carolina Press, 1999).

11. Benjamin Barber, *A Place for Us: How to Make Society Civil and Democracy Strong* (New York: Hill and Wang, 1998).

12. Carmen Sirianni and Lewis Friedland, *Civic Innovation in America: Community Empowerment, Public Policy, and the Movement for Civic Renewal* (Berkeley: University of California Press, 2001).

13. In addition to some of the texts discussed below, the Web sites of the following organizations regularly track the multitude of civil society efforts: Civic Practices Network, National Civic League, PolicyLink, Institute for Local Self-Reliance, ShelterForce, and Neighborhood Works.

14. Harry C. Boyte and Nancy N. Kari, *Building America: The Democratic Promise of Public Work* (Philadelphia: Temple University Press, 1996), p. 5.

15. See Ruy Teixeira and Joel Rogers, *America's Forgotten Majority: Why the White Working Class Still Matters* (New York: Basic Books, 2000); Theda Skocpol, *The Missing Middle: Working Families and the Future of American Social Policy* (New York: W. W. Norton, 2000); and Edward N. Wolff, *Top Heavy: The Increasing Inequality of Wealth in America and What Can Be Done About It* (New York: New Press, 1995).

16. See for example, Steven Greenhouse, "Unions, Facing Decline, Increase Their Recruiting," *New York Times* (May 30, 1997), and "Union Membership Slides Despite Increased Organizing," *New York Times* (March 22, 1998).

17. See Robert Pollin, "Living Wage, Live Action," *Nation* (November 23, 1998), pp. 15–20.

18. For a useful overview of many of these efforts that is also a brief on their behalf, see Naomi Klein, *No Logo: Taking Aim at the Brand Bullies* (New York: Picador, 1999); see also Klein, "Does Protest Need a Vision?" *Nation* (2000); and Martin Hart-Landsberg, "After Seattle: Strategic Thinking About Movement Building," *Monthly Review* (July–August 2000), p. 112.

19. See Randy Shaw, *Reclaiming America: Nike, Clean Air, and the New National Activism* (Berkeley: University of California Press, 1999), especially pp. 1–96.

20. See Archon Fung, Dara O'Rourke, and Charles Sabel, "Realizing Labor Standards: How Transparency, Competition, and Sanctions Could Improve Working Conditions Worldwide," *Boston Review* (February/March, 2001), pp. 4–10, 20.

21. Shaw, *Reclaiming America*, p. 94.

22. See my "Thinking About the Antisweatshop Movement," *Dissent* (fall 2001), pp. 36–44.

23. See Bruce A. Williams and Albert R. Matheny, *Democracy, Dialogue, and Environmental Disputes* (New Haven, CT: Yale University Press, 1995), and Andrew Szasz, *Ecopopulism: Toxic Waste and the Movement for Environmental Justice* (Minneapolis: University of Minnesota Press, 1994).

24. See, for example, Katharine Q. Seelye, "Bush Proposing to Shift Burden of Toxic Cleanups to Taxpayers," *New York Times* (February 24, 2002), A1.

25. Carmen Sirianni and Lewis Friedland, *Civic Innovation in America: Community, Empowerment, Public Policy, and the Movement for Civic Renewal* (Berkeley: University of California Press, 2001), pp. 85–137.

26. See Michael Shuman, *Going Local: Creating Self-Reliant Communities in a Global Age* (New York: Free Press, 1998); Andres Duany, Elizabeth Plater-Zyberk, and Jeff Speck, *Suburban Nation: The Rise of Sprawl and the Decline of the American Dream* (New York: North Point Press, 2000); Myron Orfield, *Metropolitics: A Regional Agenda for Community and Stability* (Washington, DC: Brookings Institution, 1997); Manuel Pastor Jr., Peter Dreier, J. Eugene Grigsby III, and Marta Lopez-Garza, *Regions That Work: How Cities and Suburbs Can Grow Together* (Minneapolis: University of Minnesota Press, 2000). Michael Sandel discusses such efforts in *Democracy's Discontent* (Cambridge, MA: Harvard University Press, 1996), pp. 334–36.

27. For an overview of such initiatives, see Lisbeth Schorr, *Common Purpose: Strengthening Families and Neighborhoods to Rebuild America* (New York: Anchor Books, 1997), Ronald F. Ferguson and William T. Dickens, eds., *Urban Problems and Community Development* (Washington, DC: Brooking Institution, 1997), and Sirianni and Friedland, *Civic Innovation*, 35–84; on the Industrial Areas Foundation,

see Sirianni and Friedland, *Civic Innovation*, pp. 43–56, and Harry Boyte, *Commonwealth: A Return to Citizen Politics* (New York: Free Press, 1989), pp. 81–126. On the Algebra Project, see my "The Calculus of Consent: The Algebra Project and Democratic Politics," *Dissent* (winter 1999).

28. Robin Garr, *Reinvesting in America* (Reading, MA: Addison-Wesley, 1995), p. 230.

29. See Mark Levinson, "Wishful Thinking," and David Moberg, "Unions and the State," in *Boston Review* (February/March 2001), pp. 13, 15.

30. "Progress in Cleaning Chesapeake Bay, But Far to Go," *New York Times* (Sunday, July 23, 2001), p. A12.

31. On these themes, see Matthew Filner, "On the Limits of Community Development: Participation, Power, and Growth in Urban America, 1965–Present" (Ph.D. Dissertation, Department of Political Science, Indiana University, August 2001).

32. Peter Edelman, *Searching for America's Heart: RFK and the Renewal of Hope* (Boston: Houghton Mifflin, 2001), p. 197.

33. For a discussion of this kind of power, see Hannah Arendt, "On Violence," in *Crises of the Republic* (New York: Harcourt, 1972), especially pp. 143–55.

34. Theda Skocpol makes this point in "Advocates Without Members," pp. 499–506. See also Christopher Beem, *The Necessity of Politics: Reclaiming American Public Life* (Chicago: University of Chicago, 1999).

35. Robert L. Woodson Jr., "A Challenge to Conservatives," *Commonsense*, vol. 1, no. 3 (summer 1994), pp. 23–25. As Christopher Beem writes: "the institutions of civil society are inherently ill suited to address some of the movement's core objectives . . . our polity is best able to achieve the goals of the civil society movement when both the state and civil society are operative and vibrant," in *The Necessity of Politics: Reclaiming American Public Life* (Chicago: University of Chicago Press, 1999), p. 3.

36. Sirianni and Friedland, *Civic Innovation*, p. 85.

37. Sirianni and Friedland, *Civic Innovation*, p. 8.

38. Sirianni and Friedland, *Civic Innovation*, pp. 1, 19.

39. Sirianni and Friedland, *Civic Innovation*, p. 9. See also p. 260, where they reiterate their view that the civic renewal "movement" has "achieved an important threshold of recognition in the media," but then note that "nonetheless, these important foundational accomplishments over a decade should not be exaggerated, nor the obstacles to further development of a broad movement underestimated."

40. Sirianni and Friedland, *Civic Innovation*, pp. 33–34.

41. See their remarks on pp. 27–71.

42. See Harry Boyte, *The Backyard Revolution: Understanding the New Citizen Movement* (Philadelphia: Temple University Press, 1980).

43. My argument here is indebted to Richard Rorty's essay "Movements and Campaigns," *Dissent* (winter 1995), pp. 55–60.

44. Sirianni and Friedland, *Civic Innovation*, pp. 272–73.

45. Sirianni and Friedland, *Civic Innovation*, pp. 264–65.

46. See Anthony Giddens, *Beyond Left and Right: The Future of Radical Politics* (Stanford: Stanford University Press, 1994) and *The Third Way* (London: Polity

Press, 1998). See also my "The Road (Not?) Taken: Anthony Giddens, The Third Way, and the Future of Social Democracy," *Dissent* (spring 2001), pp. 61–70.

47. See William A. Galston and Elaine C. Kamarck, "Five Realities That Will Shape 21st Century US Politics," reprinted in Anthony Giddens, ed., *The Global Third Way Debate* (Cambridge: Polity Press, 2001).

48. Will Marshall, "A New Fighting Faith," *New Democrat*, vol. 8, no. 5 (September/October 1996), pp. 14–15.

49. See Kenneth S. Baer, *Reinventing Democrats: The Politics of Liberalism from Clinton to Reagan* (Lawrence, KS: Kansas University Press, 2000).

50. See, for example, Don E. Eberly, ed., *Building a Community of Citizens: Civil Society in the 21st Century* (Lanham, MD: University Press of America, 1994), and Stephen Goldsmith, *The Twenty-First Century City: Resurrecting Urban America* (Lanham, MD: Rowman & Littlefield, 2002).

51. This convergence was noted in Herbert Wray et al., "The Revival of Civic Life," *US News & World Reports* (January 29, 1996). See also Craig R. Rimmerman, *The New Citizenship: Unconventional Politics, Activism, and Service* (Boulder, CO: Westview Press, 1997).

52. Sirianni and Friedland, *Civic Innovation*, p. 250. My account of the Reinventing Citizenship Project draws largely from Sirianni and Friedland's account, but also from the texts posted on the Civic Practices Network Web site.

53. This is also the chastened conclusion of Benjamin Barber, who, like Sirianni and Friedland, was an active participant in the Reinventing Citizenship Project. See Barber's recent book *The Truth of Power: Intellectual Affairs in the Clinton White House* (New York: Norton, 2001).

54. This is the theme of Benjamin DeMott's provocative *The Trouble with Friendship: Why Americans Can't Think Straight About Race* (New Haven, CT: Yale University Press, 2000).

55. Lars-Erik Nelson, "Clinton and His Enemies," *New York Review of Books* (January 20, 2000), p. 20.

56. This argument is brilliantly made by Theda Skocpol in her *Boomerang: Clinton's Health Security Effort and the Turn Against Government in U.S. Politics* (New York: W. W. Norton, 1996).

57. On this matter, see the fascinating exchange between Robert Kuttner and E. J. Dionne Jr., "Did Clinton Succeed or Fail?" *American Prospect* (August 28, 2000), pp. 42–46. See also Stephen Skowronek's discussion of Clinton's "preemptive" third way politics, in *The Politics Presidents Make: Leadership From John Adams to Bill Clinton* (Cambridge, MA: Harvard University Press, 1997), pp. 447–64.

58. This is also the argument of Ted Halsted and Michael Lind's *The Radical Center: The Future of American Politics* (New York: Doubleday, 2001).

59. See my "Faith-Based Initiatives: A Civil Society Approach," *The Good Society* (winter 2003).

60. On this theme, see Simone Chambers and Jeffrey Kopstein, "Bad Civil Society," *Political Theory*, vol. 29, no. 6 (December 2001), pp. 837–66.

61. See, for example, Stephen Carter, *Civility* (New York: Harper, 1977).

62. See, for example, Margaret Weir and Marshall Ganz, "Reconnecting People and Politics," in Stanley B. Greenberg and Theda Skocpol, eds., *The New Majority: Toward a Popular Progressive Politics* (New Haven, CT: Yale University Press, 1997).

63. For a perceptive if exaggerated argument to this effect, see Thomas Frank, *One Market Under God: Extreme Capitalism, Market Populism, and the End of Economic Democracy* (New York: Doubleday, 2000).

64. See Jay Walljasper, "Burlington, Northern Light," *Nation* (May 19, 1997), pp. 18–23; Bruce Shapiro, "Rappaport Makes the LEAP," *Nation* (September 21, 1998), pp. 27–28; Micah Sifry, "A Working Third Party," *Nation* (November 6, 2000); Harold Meyerson, "California's Progressive Mosaic," *American Prospect*, vol. 12, no. 11 (June 18, 2001); and Michael H. Shuman, "Going Local: Devolution for Progressives," *Nation* (October 12, 1998).

65. Michael Sandel, *Democracy's Discontent: America in Search of a Public Philosophy* (Cambridge, MA: Harvard University Press, 1996), pp. 324, 333, 338.

66. Sandel, *Democracy's Discontent*, pp. 324, 337, 347, 350.

67. Putnam, *Bowling Alone*, pp. 399, 401.

68. See for example William Grieder, *Who Will Tell The People* (New York: Touchstone, 1992), pp. 222–44; Harry Boyte and Nancy Kari, *Building America: The Democratic Promise of Public Work* (Philadelphia: Temple University Press, 1996), pp. 145–46; Sandel, *Democracy's Discontent*, pp. 336–38; Sirianni and Friedland, *Civic Innovation*, pp. 35–84; William Julius Wilson, *The Bridge over the Racial Divide* (Berkeley: University of California Press, 1999), pp. 85–92; and Putnam, *Bowling Alone*, p. 68.

69. Mark R. Warren, *Dry Bones Rattling: Community Building to Revitalize American Democracy* (Princeton, NJ: Princeton University Press, 2001).

70. Warren, *Dry Bones Rattling*, p. 254.

71. Warren, *Dry Bones Rattling*, pp. 256, 262.

72. Albert Camus, *The Plague*, trans. Stuart Gilbert (New York: Modern Library, 1948), p. 117; "The Myth of Sisyphus," in *The Myth of Sisyphus and Other Essays*, trans. Justin O'Brien (New York: Vintage Books, 1955), pp. 91.

Index

About the Author

Jeffrey C. Isaac is James H. Rudy Professor of Political Science and the director of the Center for the Study of Democracy at Indiana University.